Managing Compliance:

A Guide for Insurance Professionals

Dennis M. Groner, PhD., CLU, ChFC,

This publication is designed to provide accurate and authoritative information in regard to the subject matter covered. It is sold with the understanding that the publisher is not engaged in rendering legal, accounting or other professional service. If legal advice or other expert assistance is required, the services of a competent professional person should be sought.

This text is updated periodically to reflect changes in laws and regulations. To verify that you have the most recent update, you may call Dearborn at 1-800-423-4723.

© 2002 by Dearborn Financial Publishing, Inc.®
Published by Dearborn Financial Institute, Inc.®

All rights reserved. The text of this publication, or any part thereof, may not be reproduced in any manner whatsoever without written permission from the publisher.

Printed in the United States of America.

First printing, August 2002

Library of Congress Cataloging-in-Publication Data

Groner, Dennis M.
   Managing compliance : a guide for insurance professionals / Dennis M. Groner.
     p. cm.
   ISBN 0-7931-6002-2 (pbk.)
   1. Insurance companies—Management.   2. Insurance law. I. Title.
HG8075.G67 2002
368'.0068--dc21   2002011875

About the Author

Dennis Groner, Ph.D., CLU, ChFC is a recognized authority on compliance and market conduct and a a Principal in Groner & Associates, a consulting firm that provides services to companies and individuals in the financial services industry. His services include compliance and market conduct support, managing organizational change and agent and management training and education.

Mr. Groner is the author of a number of books on compliance and market conduct. In addition to *Managing Compliance: A Guide for Insurance Professionals,* he wrote *Practical Compliance for Insurance Professionals,* which was published by LIMRA International of Hartford, Connecticut. His articles regularly appear in such industry publications as Life Insurance Selling, Best's Review, GAMA's Manager's Magazine and the National Underwriter. Mr. Groner publishes a bi-monthly newsletter called *Practical Compliance.* Over 35,000 agents and managers currently receive the newsletter. He also conducts numerous industry and company workshops on compliance and market conduct and is a featured speaker at agent and management conferences and meetings.

Mr. Groner has consulted with a large number of U.S. and Canadian companies, involving all types of distribution systems, on developing and implementing compliance and market conduct assessment and monitoring procedures as well as providing agent and management training on compliance, market conduct and ethics. Several companies use his producer and agency self-assessment and company auditing programs and his agency market conduct supervision programs. He is an approved IMSA assessor and has conducted a number of IMSA assessments.

Prior to founding Groner & Associates in 1995, Mr. Groner worked for The Prudential for 17 years, where he held marketing, administrative and executive positions. Prior to joining The Prudential he worked for the Xerox Corporation. He has a Ph.D. in psychology from the University of Minnesota.

Disclaimer

Information within *Managing Compliance: A Guide for Insurance Professionals* should not be construed as, and does not constitute, the giving of legal advice. This text and its associated guides, forms, questionnaires, checklists, advisories and information are not a legal authority nor are they intended to provide specific legal advice. Such advice can be obtained only from your own legal counsel. Should you have questions about specific issues, contact your legal advisor or a company with which you are affiliated.

Every effort has been made to provide as up-to-date and accurate a guide as possible, however, the author makes no representations or warranties as to the validity or effectiveness of the conclusions, analyses, opinions or information in this text. Any and all liability arising from the guides, forms, procedures, checklists or information contained in these guides is, without limitation, disclaimed.

Dennis M. Groner,
Groner & Associates,
Livingston, NJ

Table of Contents

ACKNOWLEDGMENTS	ix
INTRODUCTION	xi
CHAPTER 1: COMPLIANCE AND MARKET CONDUCT RISK	1
What Are Compliance and Market Conduct Risk?	1
What Compliance and Market Conduct Risks Do Managers Face?	1
Why Is Being Out of Compliance Bad for Business?	3
Compliance and Market Conduct Risks from the Company's Perspective	6
A Case Study in the Costs of a Market Conduct Problem	8
CHAPTER 2: THE CHALLENGE OF CONTROLLING COMPLIANCE AND MARKET CONDUCT RISK	11
How to Control Compliance and Market Conduct Risk	11
What Compliance and Market Conduct Rules and Regulations Must Be Supervised?	12
What Is the Goal of Compliance Regulations and Laws?	16
Who Is Responsible for Managing Compliance?	17
How Companies Delegate Responsibility for Supervision	19
Why Companies Delegate Supervision	21
Potential Supervisory Challenges	22
CHAPTER 3: DEVELOPING AN EFFECTIVE COMPLIANCE AND MARKET CONDUCT SUPERVISORY SYSTEM	31
General Characteristics of an Effective Compliance and Market Conduct Supervisory System	31
Key Elements of an Effective Compliance and Market Conduct Supervisory System	32

CHAPTER 4: DEVELOPING AND COMMUNICATING EXPLICIT STANDARDS OF CONDUCT — 35

- What Are Explicit Standards of Conduct? — 35
- Why Are Explicit Standards of Conduct Needed? — 35
- How to Develop an Agency or Office Statement or Code — 36
- How to Communicate Standards of Conduct — 37
- Clear Policies and Procedures — 38
- What Information Do Agents and Administrative Staff Need? — 39
- How to Make Policies and Procedures Clear — 40
- How to Maintain Compliance and Market Conduct Policies and Procedures — 40
- Communication and Implementation of Policies and Procedures — 43

CHAPTER 5: MONITORING AND SUPERVISING COMPLIANCE AND MARKET CONDUCT — 49

- Why Are Monitoring and Supervising Compliance and Market Conduct Important? — 49
- How to Assess Current Monitoring and Supervision Systems — 49
- Potential Supervisory Challenge's — 52
- How to Create a Monitoring and Supervisory System — 55
- Key Specific Monitoring Issues — 63
- Monitoring Suitability — 63
- Monitoring Replacements — 68
- Monitoring Persistency — 77
- Monitoring Sales Material Use — 80
- Monitoring Proper Disclosure — 83
- Monitoring Proper Completion of Applications and Forms — 86
- Monitoring Money Laundering — 87
- Monitoring Licensing — 89
- General Indicators of Potential Market Conduct and Compliance Problems — 92
- Errors to Avoid in Supervising Compliance and Market Conduct — 93
- How to Effectively Implement Enhancements to Supervisory Systems — 95

CHAPTER 6: TAKING CORRECTIVE ACTION ON POTENTIAL COMPLIANCE AND MARKET CONDUCT ISSUES — 99

- Why Must the General Agent or Agency Manager Take Corrective Action? — 99
- Which Issues Should Be Handled by a General Agent or Agency Manager? — 99
- How Should a General Agent or Agency Manager Take Corrective Action on Possible Compliance Issues? — 101
- How Should a General Agent or Agency Manager Handle Company-Instigated Investigations? — 102
- Which Corrective Actions Should Be Taken? — 103
- How Should the General Agent or Agency Manager Make Certain the Mistake Is Not Repeated? — 105
- What If the Employee Must Be Terminated? — 107
- Tips on Taking Action — 109

CHAPTER 7: HOW TO INTEGRATE COMPLIANCE AND MARKET CONDUCT INTO MANAGING FOR SUCCESS — 113

Recruiting and Selecting New Agents	113
Recruiting and Selecting Experienced Agents	114
Training	117
Communication	119
Coaching and Counseling	121
Supervising Productivity	123
Motivating	124
Agency Operations	125

CHAPTER 8: MARKET CONDUCT AND COMPLIANCE EXAMINATIONS AND AUDITS — 127

Overview of Exams and Audits and Their Purpose	127
How a General Agent or Agency Manager Can Make Company Market Conduct Examinations Effective	133
How a General Agent or Agency Manager Can Prepare for an Examination or Audit	134
Communication Issues Involved in an Examination	135
How an Agency or Office Can Cooperate with Examiners	136
How Companies Conduct Examinations	137
What Examiners Look for	138
How Companies Share Examination Results with the General Agent or Agency Manager	139
NASD Requirements for Audits and Examinations	140
Registered Representative Examinations	141
How to Periodically Examine Agent and Agency or Office Compliance and Market Conduct	142
How to Review Case Files	144
How to Review Computer Files	144
Reviewing Web Sites	146
Tips on Conducting Agent Examinations	147
In Closing	148

**APPENDIX A: EXAMPLE OF A SUPERVISORY
RESPONSIBILITY MATRIX** 149

**APPENDIX B: EXAMPLES OF COMPLIANCE-RELATED
ACTIVITIES** 153

APPENDIX C: SAMPLE STATEMENT OF AGENT CONDUCT 161

APPENDIX D: THE CONCEPT OF ETHICAL LEADERSHIP 167

**APPENDIX E: BEING OUT OF COMPLIANCE IS BAD
FOR BUSINESS—AN AGENT'S PERSPECTIVE** 171

APPENDIX F: LISTING OF POTENTIAL EXAMINATION POINTS 173

**APPENDIX G: SAMPLE OF AN NASD EXAMINATION
RECORD FORM** 179

APPENDIX H: SAMPLE CASE OR FILE REVIEW CHECKLIST 187

Acknowledgments

I wish to express thanks to the following people for their help and encouragement in writing this book. Several of the following individuals reviewed various chapters and made significant improvements in them:

- Jim Buddle, General Electric Capital

- Jeffrey Cooper, Great American Financial Resources, Inc.

- Andrew Coriselli, JD, CLU, Manulife Financial

- Kenneth Daniels, JD, CLU, IFG Network Securities, Inc.

- Kay Doughty, JD, Doughty Consulting

- Thomas Horack, John Hancock Financial

- Stephen Leimberg, JD, CLU, Leimberg Associates

- Imants Saksons, CLU, Sun Life (USA)

- Gary Schulte, CLU, MET Life

- Steve Torretto, JD, CPA, CLU, ChFC, Pacific Life

I would also like to thank my loving wife, Barbara, for her support throughout the writing of this book. Her encouragement motivated me to complete it when faced with other projects, deadlines and duties. She was always willing to lend an ear to listen to an idea or make a suggestion on how to overcome an obstacle.

— Dennis M. Groner

Introduction

WHAT IS THE PURPOSE OF THIS BOOK?

General agents and agency managers are responsible for supervising the compliance and market conduct of their agents. They are responsible for different tasks, but, in general, managers are responsible for the compliance and market conduct of the agents and administrative staff that they directly or indirectly supervise. This general responsibility usually is defined specifically in job descriptions or contract provisions.

The overall goal of this book is to help general agents and agency managers carry out these responsibilities effectively and efficiently. Specifically, we hope:

- to help general agents and agency managers become sensitive to the compliance and market conduct risks associated with their responsibilities in supervising other insurance professionals;

- to provide general agents and agency managers with processes that will help them manage those risks;

- to provide general agents and agency managers with guidance for implementing those processes;

- to provide general agents and agency managers with ideas for integrating compliance into their normal agency processes and procedures;

- to help general agents and agency managers who have relationships with several companies to develop an integrated system for meeting the requirements of each of those companies; and

- to help agency managers who work for a company with comprehensive systems and controls to understand how to maximize these systems and their rationale.

Periodically, we also will focus on the impact of market conduct and compliance from a company perspective. Providing this perspective may help general agents and agency managers better understand how and why companies react to market conduct and compliance issues.

1

Compliance and Market Conduct Risk

■ WHAT ARE COMPLIANCE AND MARKET CONDUCT RISK?

General agents and agency managers are increasingly being held accountable by companies and regulators for the market conduct and compliance of the agents who work for them.

According to both managers of captive agents (agency managers) and managers of independent agents (for example, managing general agents), the work of monitoring and supervising agents has increased as companies have shifted much of the responsibility for supervising the conduct of agents to their immediate supervisors. In some cases, this manager is the registered principal and may be responsible for endorsing the suitability of variable product applications, reviewing correspondence and conducting periodic audits and annual audits. Registered principals' responsibility is mandated by NASD guidelines, which all broker-dealers must follow.

But even for nonregistered products, companies consider managers their first line of defense against market conduct problems and hold them responsible for supervising and monitoring their agents' market conduct.

■ WHAT COMPLIANCE AND MARKET CONDUCT RISKS DO MANAGERS FACE?

General agents and agency managers face the following risks:

- Improper actions by administrative and marketing support staff in support of the general agent, agency manager or agent, for example:

    – failing to properly notify the agent or company of a client complaint;

    – making changes in applications without the knowledge of the client or agent;

    – soliciting the sale of insurance without proper licenses;

- providing advice on the investment aspects of variable products without having the proper registration and license; or

- misrepresenting the features, costs and benefits of products to clients.

- Improper actions of agents, for example:

    - misrepresenting or failing to disclose the features, costs and benefits of products to clients;

    - providing unsuitable recommendations to clients regarding products and services;

    - using unapproved sales materials;

    - failing to inform a company that a proposed sale involves the replacement of a current life insurance, annuity or long-term care product;

    - improperly completing applications; or

    - failing to follow company procedures regarding maintaining records, files and documentation.

- Failure to supervise agents and support staff, for example:

    - knowingly allowing an agent to submit unsuitable business;

    - ignoring or minimizing the seriousness of agent misconduct;

    - conducting a cursory or inadequate audit of agent practices or not following company procedures regarding the detail required for an audit;

    - endorsing applications without adequately evaluating them;

    - alerting agents of surprise audits or inspections; or

    - knowingly allowing agents to circumvent company rules and regulations.

- Improper actions of the general agent or agency manager, for example:

    - attempting to hide the use of unapproved sales materials;

    - hiring an agent with the express intention of helping the agent replace insurance placed with the agent's prior company;

    - developing marketing programs that lead to improper market conduct of the agents who use them; or

    - not providing timely feedback to a company regarding a client complaint or investigation.

Some markets and products are more susceptible to market conduct problems than others. A general agent or agency manager should be sensitive to the risks involved in the work of the people he or she manages and the products and services they offer. For example, agents who replace life insurance policies or use the accumulated values in life insurance to sell additional life insurance policies or annuities, agents who replace annuities, especially when they are subject to surrender and withdrawal charges and agents who sell life insurance or annuities to seniors or who do work site marketing are susceptible to market conduct problems.

These types of compliance and market conduct risks raise several key points:

- For general agents and agency managers, errors of omission—ignoring improper behavior or failing to take action—are as serious as errors of commission—taking improper action.

- The scope of the general agent and agency manager's exposure is multiplied by the number of agents, administrative staff and second line managers for which he or she has responsibility and by the type of product agents sell and the markets in which they sell.

- General agents and managers must focus not only on the propriety of the actions agents, administrative staff and managers take with clients, which is the typical focus of compliance and market conduct, but also on how they comply with company policies and procedures. Failing to carry out company policies or to follow company procedures can lead to serious compliance problems whether or not the client is affected directly.

The compliance-savvy general agent or agency manager knows that significant personal and professional costs are associated with these risks. In our society, many professions have been targeted by disgruntled consumers and their legal counsel. The insurance industry is no exception. Over the last several years, some of the most prestigious insurance companies have found themselves in the crosshairs of regulators or plaintiffs' counsel.

Clients and their attorneys believe insurance companies are easy targets for significant settlements. To get to an insurance company, however, a plaintiff must go through the agent who sold the contract. When an agent is involved, the general agent or agency manager is also involved because a manager can be accused of improperly supervising the agent.

Too often, agents and their general agents or agency managers are just "speed bumps" that plaintiffs' counsel must get over to reach the insurance company. The specific accusation is irrelevant. The result is that the agent is named in a suit along with the general agent or agency manager and the company the agent represented. The client complains to regulators to bolster the case and broaden the effect it has on the agent and the company.

■ WHY IS BEING OUT OF COMPLIANCE BAD FOR BUSINESS?

Lawsuits and compliance and market conduct problems are costly for insurance companies in a number of ways. This is true whether a general agent or agency manager is involved or simply an agent or member of the administrative support staff—guilt by association is difficult to avoid. Following are some of the improper market conduct costs of which general agents or agency managers should become more aware.

Agency Productivity

The productivity of agents involved in market conduct problems typically suffers. The negative impact on an agent's self-confidence, productivity and reputation can lead to decreases in productivity as drastic as 30 to 50 percent. Even agents who are not directly involved in the market conduct problem, however, can suffer from the negative impact on agency reputation, disruptions in agency operations and efficiency, loss of focus, fear of creating some of the same problems or other worries. The smaller the agency, the greater the negative impact a market conduct problem can have on agency production.

Reputation

Reputation is a key ingredient in a general agent or agency manager's success. It is critical when recruiting or retaining agents and second line managers. Reference centers may be leery of recommending your agency to potential agents if they have concerns about your reputation. General agents and agency managers who do personal business may find that their clients are concerned about doing business with them because of an agent's reputation for questionable practices.

Favorable name recognition in a community is difficult to gain and easy to lose—and in some local communities, if your reputation is sullied, you might as well close up shop. Even when the agent, administrative staff person, general agent or agency manager is found to have done nothing wrong, accusations of misconduct are hard to erase from people's minds. Settling cases out of court may make legal sense, but because this strategy doesn't decide right from wrong, it can give the public the impression that there really was a problem.

Usually a legal action involving market conduct cannot be kept secret from other professionals or the community. For example, a company may feel required to survey an agent's other clients to see if similar problems are present, or the state may request that other clients be interviewed to determine if the problem was widespread. The company may have to interview clients, agents or administrative staff. Although they will not tell these people what they are investigating, it sometimes is apparent from the questions asked.

Time

Nothing eats up productive time like a market conduct problem. A general agent's or agency manager's time is taken up by responding to written requests for information from the company or state regulators, interviewing agents, administrative staff or clients and the company's legal counsel, reviewing files, preparing for and giving depositions, coaching and counseling agents, and other tasks. Often this work cannot be delegated, so the general agent or agency manager must spend his or her time carrying out these activities. Cases often take a long time to run their course—some lasting for years. Time is spent reviewing material over and over again as each new stage in the legal process takes place. Once this time is spent on unproductive activities, it cannot be reclaimed.

Trust in Other Agents or Administrative Staff

When a trusted agent or administrative staff person becomes embroiled in a market conduct or compliance problem, it raises questions about the motivations of other agents or staff. General agents and agency managers who have experienced such incidents can become cynical about their co-workers and employees. This potential lack of trust is more damaging when the agent or administrative staff person claims that the general agent or agency manager contributed to the problem, for example, by failing to provide training or supervision. Sometimes general agents or agency managers overreact because it can be so disheartening to find that his or her trust was misplaced. This level of distrust can undermine the team spirit and loyalty of the other agents and administrative staff in the agency.

Company Trust in the General Agent or Agency Manager

When a company suspects a general agent or agency manager of having done something wrong or of not paying close enough attention to market conduct issues, it must scrutinize the way that agency operates. Companies also can be accused of failing to properly supervise employees, so they become cautious of general agents or agency managers whose agents have been the target of market conduct complaints or problems. Companies want to be able to demonstrate that they provide the proper level of supervision when dealing with potential problem agencies. Sometimes companies put an agency on a watch list and scrutinize its operation. For example, they may screen new policy applications more carefully or may exercise greater care in reviewing candidates for appointment. They may be more willing to survey clients or client transactions, such as loans and withdrawals. They also may be less willing to make exceptions to company procedures for general agents or agency managers who have had market conduct problems.

Associates' Confidence and Trust

If an agent, general agent or agency manager is the target of improper conduct charges, other insurance, financial planning, legal or business professionals may lose their confidence in the agent's advice. Would you want to work on a case with someone accused of having improper market conduct? Associates may seek a second opinion when dealing with an agent who is under suspicion or may be reluctant to work with agents in an agency with market conduct problems. A lack of trust can undermine the functioning of any agency by making members of the agency distrustful of their associates.

If the Unthinkable Happens

When a general agent or agency manager is found to have done something wrong, it heightens all of the negative effects discussed above. Today, more than ever before, companies are taking a more aggressive stance in disciplining general agents and agency managers who have acted improperly. They may terminate a contract, limit privileges, assess fines and so forth. If a variable product is involved, the company must report the misconduct to the National Association of Securities Dealers (NASD). The company may fine the agent, suspend NASD registration for a period of time or terminate the contract. The NASD could also fine the manager. A U-5 form, which goes on the general agent's or agency manager's record with the

NASD, must be filed for many types of misconduct. Even if the general agent or agency manager maintains his or her NASD registration, he or she still must find a broker-dealer to work for. Broker-dealers are increasingly reluctant to hire anyone who has had market conduct problems. A general agent or agency manager who has had market conduct problems causes a company to think twice about extending a contract. In today's marketplace, being unable to sell registered products could end some general agents' or agency managers' careers.

■ COMPLIANCE AND MARKET CONDUCT RISKS FROM THE COMPANY'S PERSPECTIVE

Based on the legal concept of *agency,* companies often are held responsible for the actions their agents and managers take. Consequently, insurance companies have become very proactive about market conduct and compliance issues. They work hard to communicate their policies and procedures and clearly specify appropriate and inappropriate actions. This is done to help agents and managers avoid acting improperly and also to provide the company with a strong defense against legal action. By demonstrating that they carried out their responsibility to communicate proper procedures to the agent and manager, companies hope to shift responsibility onto them. By describing appropriate market conduct, the company can claim that the improper actions of the agent and manager were due to the agent or manager's failure to follow proper procedure.

Because companies are held accountable for supervising and monitoring the actions of their agents, they have developed procedures and processes to carry out this responsibility. Their goal is twofold: to identify potential problems and resolve them before they become serious, and to defend against accusations that they failed to supervise properly. By combining written procedures, communications, education programs and supervisory policies and procedures, some companies have created a strong defense to protect them from liability in legal action involving their agents and managers' market conduct and compliance.

The cost of improper market conduct and compliance to companies can be great. Legal issues can consume significant company time and energy. Class action suits have exacted a high cost in legal fees, settlement costs and reputation. The number and cost of individual suits have also increased because of public awareness of potential improper market conduct. Legal costs and settlements have risen as clients have become more willing to sue and their counsels' knowledge of how to sue successfully has increased.

There seems to be clear relationship between the number of consumer complaints regulators receive and the frequency and depth of regulator audits. Regulators appear to scrutinize the practices of companies that are the target of consumer complaints and suits. Regulators' audits often require a significant expenditure of company resources because it takes time to collect and provide the information requested. The company is responsible for the cost of the auditors.

Regulators have attempted to communicate the seriousness of their concerns about market conduct and compliance by increasing the frequency and magnitude of their fines over the last several years. Sometimes regulators require that the company change procedures as a result of market conduct problems. The cost of these

> **ILL. 1.1 ■ *The Concept of Agency***
>
> The concept of agency dictates that an agent-principal relationship exists between two parties where one of those parties (the principal) gives the other party (the principal's agent) the authority to act on its behalf and subject to its control.
>
> When an insurance company appoints someone to act on its behalf, that is, as an agent of the company, it assumes responsibility for the actions that agent takes on its behalf. The authority of the company's agent can bind the company to the actions of the agent. If the agent makes a mistake or commits an error, the principal often is held responsible. Companies are, therefore, rightly concerned about the market conduct and compliance of their agents, producers and managers.
>
> When used in the context of the concept of agency, the term *agent* has a specific legal meaning. It also has a colloquial meaning, that is, someone who holds a life insurance or health insurance license and is appointed by an insurance company. The term is also sometimes used to differentiate between an employee, or *captive agent*, versus an *independent producer*.
>
> Some managers incorrectly assume that because their contract with an insurance company uses the term *broker, independent producer, managing general agent,* and so forth, that they somehow are not bound by the concept of agency. A manager who has an agent-principal relationship with an insurance company, regardless of their job description or title, is an agent and is bound by the concept of agency and its duties and responsibilities.
>
> Some insurance managers and professionals operate as independent contractors instead of agents. Another area of law deals with their duties and responsibilities. To determine your status, you should begin by carefully reading your contract. Some contracts specifically state that the general agent or agency manager is an agent of the company. You can also contact the legal counsel of the insurance company you contract with for their opinion on your status. Finally, you can contact your personal legal counsel and ask them to review your contract to determine if you are an agent in the legal sense.

changes, including reprogramming systems or reprinting materials, can be significant. They also can detract from the company's marketing efforts.

Clearly, it is in a company's best interest to avoid giving regulators the impression that it is not concerned about compliance and market conduct.

Anyone concerned about the productivity and profitability of life insurance companies must consider the cost of improper market conduct. Money spent on resolving market conduct problems is an unproductive use of company capital. Spending resources to avoid market conduct problems costs less and has a more positive effect than attempting to resolve them after the fact.

A CASE STUDY IN THE COSTS OF A MARKET CONDUCT PROBLEM

Dave Smith's agency was in an upscale suburb of a major Mid Atlantic city. He had been building the agency for five years and had 10 agents working with him. Together they did approximately $2 million in combined commissions in 2001. Typically, Dave hired two or three new agents each year and had been growing his agency by at least two net agents each year for the last three years.

In 2000, Dave hired Alan Jones, an experienced agent who had worked for several companies in the past, including Big Eastern Mutual and Midwestern Independent. Dave had learned the business working for Big Eastern Mutual when he first came into the business. He met Alan when he was a regional sales manager there.

In the first six months Alan was hired, he began replacing business he had originally written when at Big Eastern Mutual and Midwestern Independent. He placed them with several of the companies that Dave's agency had relationships with, for example, ABC Insurance, Eastern Established Brokerage and West Coast Brokerage Company.

Alan submitted the proper company forms and Dave reviewed them in keeping with the policy of each company to which the business was submitted. When he reviewed the applications, Dave asked Alan if they were appropriate replacements, and Alan assured him that they were.

Over the course of the first year that Alan worked in Dave's Agency, he replaced a total of 30 permanent life insurance policies and 10 annuities. The policies were placed with a number of different companies.

Alan's prior companies, Big Eastern Mutual and Midwestern Independent Insurance, contacted the replacing companies and questioned whether the replacements were appropriate. At about the same time, one of the replacing companies, ABC Insurance, received written complaints from two of Alan's clients who had replaced their policies.

ABC Insurance asked Dave if the replacements were appropriate. He talked with Alan, who explained that his clients were being harassed by the manager of Midwestern Independent who was trying to conserve the business he was losing. Alan claimed that his clients were being told things about the replacement that weren't true. He blamed the local manager from Midwestern Independent for instigating the complaints.

Dave responded in a letter to ABC Insurance that he had discussed the replacements with Alan and that to the best of his knowledge they were appropriate.

However, over the next six months, several more of Alan's clients complained that they were not aware of the negative impact of the replacements they had accepted. ABC Insurance received a total of four complaints, and Midwestern Independent a total of three. Dave was repeatedly asked to investigate and determine whether the replacements were appropriate. He found himself spending more and more time documenting, interviewing and writing letters to these companies about the cases.

He counseled Alan regarding additional replacements, but Alan kept on replacing his prior business, which further strained their relationship. The regional vice president of ABC Insurance called Dave and advised him that the company was concerned about the business he was submitting. At about the same time, ABC's underwriting became slower for all of Dave's agents. Every agent's applications were scrutinized and numerous questions were asked. Several of Dave's agents criticized him for hiring Alan. They felt that he had poisoned the good relationship they had with ABC Insurance.

One of the disgruntled clients hired an attorney, filed a complaint with the state insurance commissioner and sued the agent, manager and company for misrepresentation and fraud. Dave was shocked when he was notified of the suit. He had always been proud of the fact that no one in his agency had ever had a written customer complaint. Now he had several complaints on his record and was being sued. He was ready to terminate his relationship with Alan, but he was counseled by ABC Insurance that it was not in anyone's best interest to do that at the present time.

Alan steadfastly refused to accept any blame for the replacements, claiming that they were appropriate, that he had submitted the required forms and that Dave and ABC Insurance had reviewed them and accepted them.

Dave notified his E&O carrier, who provided legal counsel. Alan notified his E&O carrier, who provided legal counsel. ABC obtained local legal counsel to handle the case and also involved its home office legal department. To Dave it seemed that he was constantly being asked questions by attorneys. To prepare for the case, he had to collect information and meet with several people from ABC and their local counsel. For two weeks he was unable to pay much attention to the agency or his own clients.

Perhaps that was why it came as a total surprise to him when two of his agents informed him that they were going to leave his agency and set themselves up separately. They felt that they needed to go off on their own to continue to grow their practices. However, Dave heard later from another agent that really they were concerned that their reputations might be hurt by their association with Dave's agency because of Alan.

Things seemed to quiet down for a time as the attorneys built their cases. ABC tried to settle, but they and the plaintiff could not agree on a settlement. During this time, Alan's business dried up. Dave believed that Alan was placing business with other companies, but he really wanted to have nothing to do with him, so he didn't care. At the same time, the production of some of the other agents declined. One agent he had recruited the year before, the daughter of a good friend, went into a slump. Because of the case and all of his other distractions, Dave did not have enough time to spend with her to help her out of it. She then decided to take a job in another industry. Within six months his agency's production had dropped 40%. He was concerned about covering his office expenses and seriously considering letting one of his administrative people go. Months before his problems had begun, he had planned to move to better office space, but now those plans were postponed indefinitely.

Dave did not think that things could get worse, but he learned from a friend about rumors circulating that he was having legal problems because of fraudulent sales. Dave had always done a significant amount of personal production, but he was embarrassed to call on his clients because of the case. Recruiting new agents seemed out of the question. Though he knew he had not done anything wrong, he felt guilty.

When Dave heard that ABC and the plaintiff had settled, he was relieved. The company recaptured the overrides and commissions on that sale, but he had expected that. At one point he thought ABC would terminate his contract with them, but they agreed not to if he would attend training sessions on compliance and market conduct. Alan terminated his relationship with Dave and ABC. Dave was not sorry to see him clean out his office and leave.

Dave finally thought his troubles were over. However, the law firm representing the plaintiff also had been retained by two of Alan's other clients who had replaced their policies. Dave wondered when it would all end.

2
The Challenge of Controlling Compliance and Market Conduct Risk

■ **HOW TO CONTROL COMPLIANCE AND MARKET CONDUCT RISK**

Market conduct risk is an integral part of doing business in today's marketplace; and although it cannot be eliminated, it can be controlled by reducing the likelihood that conduct and compliance issues will arise and by lessening the severity of their negative consequences (fines, legal actions, and so forth) when they do.

General agents and agency managers can reduce such risks by utilizing supervisory systems, processes and procedures. Supervisory systems should be designed to accomplish the following:

- provide agents and administrative staff with information and training on what constitutes proper and improper market conduct behavior and compliance;

- maintain up-to-date company, state and NASD guidelines and regulations;

- integrate market conduct and compliance procedures into normal operations and procedures;

- monitor agent and administrative staff actions on a regular basis to identify problems quickly;

- identify instances in which agents and administrative staff fail to follow company procedures properly;

- take quick and appropriate action if improprieties are identified;

- document supervisory procedures and processes;

- maintain appropriate records and data;

- demonstrate the consistent and active use of supervisory procedures;

- periodically review supervisory procedures to ensure that they identify improper market conduct and compliance actions; and

- update and modify supervisory procedures to meet changing needs.

For companies, other aspects of developing and maintaining a supervisory system for reducing compliance and market conduct risk include the following:

- evaluating the potential compliance and market conduct issues raised by their products and determining ways to reduce their potential impact;

- monitoring administrative procedures, such as compliant handling, replacement monitoring, licensing, sales material review, and so forth, to identify whether they meet regulatory standards;

- providing adequate resources and training to the staff involved in compliance and market conduct supervision and monitoring, including information on law, compliance, auditing, and so forth;

- conducting periodic audits and examinations of company processes to identify if they continue to comply with regulatory standards; and

- periodically evaluating and reporting to top management on the state of policies, procedures and processes used by the company to control compliance and market conduct risk.

A compliance and market conduct supervisory system helps reduce the risk of improper behavior and actions. If improprieties occur, the system should provide early warning so actions can be taken to minimize their seriousness. When improprieties do occur, the use of a supervisory system provides evidence that the general agent or agency manager did not condone or facilitate improprieties and that the agent or administrative staff person is fully responsible for their own actions.

Guidance on how to develop and implement a compliance and market conduct supervisory system will be provided in a later section of this guide.

WHAT COMPLIANCE AND MARKET CONDUCT RULES AND REGULATIONS MUST BE SUPERVISED?

State and federal regulations are designed to ensure that consumers are treated fairly and equitably by anyone who transacts business in the insurance industry. Regulations and laws provide a framework for proper oversight by regulators and companies and identify sanctions for improper conduct. It is important for insurance professionals to understand and appreciate the role state and federal regulations play in protecting consumers. These are the regulations that govern how we must conduct ourselves. Supervisors of agents have the responsibility to ensure that their agents follow those regulations.

> **ILL. 2.1 ■ *Regulatory Environment***
>
> The current status of state regulation of the insurance business is under examination as a result of the recently enacted Gramm-Leach-Bliley (GLB) Act of 1999. It is unclear at present how state regulations will adapt to fit federal statutes. Though state regulators have demonstrated that they can react quickly to the GLB Act by putting in place the privacy regulations it requires, it is still too early to tell how the federal government and states will work together to provide industry oversight. For the foreseeable future, insurance professionals will have to pay close attention to the regulatory environment as it adapts to new federal and state statutes and regulations.

The following is a brief overview of the various sources of rules, regulations and laws governing the sale of life insurance, annuities and securities.

State Regulations

Each state is responsible for regulating the sale of insurance products in its jurisdiction. Regulations are based on the laws, statutes and regulations it has formulated and adopted. States typically have regulations dealing with all aspects of insurance sales, including licensing, fair competition, advertising, replacements, claim and compliant handing and the filing of applications and forms. State laws regarding insurance can be found in the following sources: state statutes, state administrative codes, insurance commission bulletins, attorney general opinions and case law. Insurance regulations can be found in consumer protection statutes, statutes specific to insurance, fair trade statutes, etc.

The National Association of Insurance Commissions (NAIC) is a voluntary organization of state regulators. Though they provide states with model regulations, these models are not laws—they serve only as guidance for the states in developing their own regulations. Even though many states adopt NAIC regulation models (for advertising, illustrations, replacements, etc.), there is a great deal of variability between states' regulations. Compliance and market conduct standards and how one meets them differs greatly from state to state. Appropriate market conduct in some states would be considered improper in others.

Most state insurance regulations are the result of legislation passed over the years. Few states have well-organized, up-to-date regulations for all areas of insurance. As new products are introduced, states develop regulations for their sale. For example, when universal life products became widespread in the late 1970s and 1980s, states adopted regulations that addressed them. Newer regulations often deal with issues that are not covered by existing regulations because the issues did not exist when the older regulations were formulated. Sometimes the complexity of the issue delays the NAIC and the states from developing new regulations. For example, the NAIC developed, and a large number of states adopted, regulations regarding illustrations for traditional products in the mid to late 1990s. However, similar models for illustrations of variable products still have not been finalized.

Until the Gramm-Leach-Bliley Act of 1999, states were not required to have consistent standards. Under Gramm-Leach-Bliley, they now are required to have consistent licensing and privacy standards. However, the wide differences in state regulations means that insurance professionals must pay close attention to the regulations of every state in which they do business.

State laws regulating securities are called *blue-sky laws*. Most states have regulations that require firms and their representatives to be registered before transacting securities-related business in the state. Many states also require that securities products be registered with the state before being sold.

Key Federal Regulations

Securities Act of 1933

This act marked the beginning of the federal government's modern regulation of the securities industry. Its purpose is to ensure that the public is fully informed about a security and the company that issues it. Its goal is to protect the public from fraud and misrepresentation by requiring full and fair disclosure of important information about the security, hence its full title, Truth in Securities Act. The act mandates a process for registering new issues of a security, requires the creation of a document that provides full disclosure about the security and the prospectus and mandates that a current prospectus be delivered during the sale of a security.

Securities Exchange Act of 1934

The purpose of this act is to ensure organized markets for the sale of securities and establish reporting requirements, financial standards and controls over securities transactions. Its goal is to protect consumers from market manipulation, deception, misrepresentation and other improper conduct. It created the Securities Exchange Commission (SEC) to enforce laws pertaining to the securities industry and gives it the authority to investigate companies and their representatives for improper conduct and discipline them by imposing a range of sanctions, such as fines, censure, suspension and permanent disbarment.

Maloney Act of 1938

This act was an amendment to the Securities Exchange Act of 1934. Its goal is to allow the securities industry to set up self-regulating organizations to supervise and police the conduct of its members, for example, the NASD, whose purpose is to promote the securities business, standardize processes and procedures, encourage high standards of ethical conduct and supervise the market conduct of its members.

The NASD has two subsidiaries—the Nasdaq Stock Market, Inc. (Nasdaq) and NASD Regulation (NASDR), Inc. The Nasdaq is a stock exchange that is similar to the New York Stock Exchange, but deals in the stock of generally smaller, less-established companies, sometimes referred to as *over the counter* (OTC) securities. NASDR was established in 1996 to supervise the operation of the broker-dealers who are members of the NASD. The NASDR has developed a set of regulations to govern the market conduct of its members—NASD conduct rules. These require broker-dealers and their representatives to conduct themselves ethically and fairly, so that the public is protected from market conduct abuses and cover many of the same areas as state regulations, for example, advertising, licensing, compliant handling and supervisory responsibility. The NASDR investigates its members' market conduct and can sanction and discipline its members and their representatives.

The NASDR oversees the sale of variable life insurance, variable annuities and mutual funds. These products are called registered products and can be sold only by registered representatives of a broker-dealer who is a member of the NASDR. The popularity of these products means that the majority of life insurance professionals are registered representatives and are governed by the NASDR's rules.

Investment Company Act of 1940

This act regulates mutual funds and other investment companies, including investments underlying variable life insurance and annuities. Its goal is to require disclosure of information regarding the investments and their management so that the public has complete and accurate information on which to base their investment decisions. For example, the managers of an investment company must disclose any conflicts of interest, including any work as managers and directors for another company or individual investors.

Investment Advisors Act of 1940

This act requires individuals engaged in the business of providing recommendations and advice about securities to be registered with the SEC and to comply with statutory standards and guidelines. This act provides the regulations regarding Registered Investment Advisors (RIAs). Its goal is to protect the public by ensuring that individuals who are compensated for their advice are qualified, provide full disclosure of their background, qualifications and compensation arrangements and are supervised and monitored regarding their conduct. The act also mandates record-keeping, reporting and anti-fraud duties for RIAs and imposes restrictions on how RIAs provide advice and execute trades.

Gramm-Leach-Bliley Act of 1999

Recent developments in bank and insurance company mergers, as well as the sale of life insurance by banks, have somewhat clouded the question of who has jurisdiction over life insurance sales. Banks registered at the federal level are supervised by the Office of the Comptroller of the Currency. Insurance companies are not registered on the federal level and, therefore, no such body or office exists for insurance companies. Banks also are subject to state regulations.

In the areas of licensing and privacy protection, the Gramm-Leach-Bliley Act requires states to develop uniform standards. By mid 2001, over three quarters of the states had enacted appropriate privacy regulations. It is unclear at the present time if additional federal legislation will be enacted that impacts the states' regulation of the sale of life insurance. Until this issue has been resolved, the states' and NASDR's rules and regulations are the key standards by which the insurance industry should operate.

WHAT IS THE GOAL OF COMPLIANCE REGULATIONS AND LAWS?

The states and the NASDR are motivated by concern that the products and services provided by the insurance industry might be misrepresented to the public. The purpose of many insurance regulations is to protect the public from being misled or deceived into making unwise and potentially harmful decisions about their finances.

The states' concern was clearly demonstrated by the 1994 case in which Metropolitan Life Insurance agents in Florida were found to have engaged in widespread improper sales practices.

The state regulators' concerns were echoed in the 1997 Multi-State Task Force of Insurance Regulators report on market conduct abuses by the Prudential Insurance Company of America. According to the report:

> *The abuses reviewed by the Task Force involved more than simply a few rogue agents or isolated instances of improper sales presentations. The Task Force found that in many cases, Prudential's field force, selling to consumers throughout the country, failed to comply with both the company's directives and the states' requirements with respect to replacements. Prudential did not exercise the degree of control and oversight that the public and the regulators have a right to expect from an insurance company.* *

This report identified the following problems:

- failure to identify life insurance as the product being sold (20 million pieces distributed);

- permitting producers to use unauthorized or misleading titles such as financial planner or insurance consultant;

- misleading statements or omissions regarding taxes;

- use of unsupported or undocumented statistics;

- use of misleading or deceptive terminology; and

- use of misleading material in order to market a program known as "Personal Pension Plan." Although the material did identify life insurance as the funding vehicle, the state believed the material and presentation stressed the plan as a tax-favored retirement mechanism. **

These cases serve as an example of what can go wrong when a company does not exercise stringent controls over the approval and use of sales materials and sales practices. In addition to the costs of fines, penalties and refunds, reputation and

---

* New Jersey Department of Banking and Insurance News Release, July 9, 1996
** *Multi-State Task Force and Multi-State Market Conduct Examination of The Prudential Insurance Company of America,* July 9, 1996, pp. 66-67

> **ILL. 2.2 ■ *Good Intentions Aren't Enough***
>
> The vast majority of insurance professionals do not consciously misrepresent themselves, their company or their products and services. Misunderstanding state and NASDR rules and regulations, however, may lead to compliance violations. Good intentions or ignorance, however, are a poor defense against allegations of misconduct and wrongdoing.

credibility are lost with the public, which translates into lost sales and hampered recruiting efforts.

■ WHO IS RESPONSIBLE FOR MANAGING COMPLIANCE?

Everyone is responsible for managing compliance. The agent, manager and company all share responsibility for proper market conduct and compliance. However, for general agents and agency managers, some aspects to this question are particularly important to note.

Though supervision is assumed to be the responsibility of the general agent or agency manager, sometimes it is not clear how that responsibility is assigned.

Among regulators, the NASDR is the clearest in specifying its supervisory requirements:

> *Each member shall establish and maintain a system to supervise the activities of each registered representative and associated person that is reasonably designed to achieve compliance with applicable securities laws and regulations, and with the Rules of this Association.**

Member in this context means the broker-dealer who is a member of the NASD.

The NASDR requires a member's supervisory system to provide, at a minimum, the following:

- written supervisory procedures;

- designation of an office of supervisory jurisdiction (OSJ);

- designation of registered principals in each OSJ and non-OSJ branch to carry out supervision;

---

* NASD Notice to Members, 98-38

> **ILL. 2.3 ▪ *The Agent Is Responsible for Market Conduct***
>
> Agents ultimately must bear responsibility for their own market conduct and compliance. Though they can be excused to some extent by a lack of training or information, ignorance of rules and regulations is a weak defense for market conduct and compliance errors. As licensed professionals, agents should be aware of the rules and regulations they must follow. The agent should rely on the general agent or agency manager for advice, guidance and support, but he or she should never assume that the responsibility for proper market conduct and compliance belong to the general agent, agency manager or company alone. This is true even for agents who work in a captive distribution system. Agents need to exercise self-supervision regardless of their relationship with the companies whose products they sell.

- assignment of each representative to a registered principal for supervisory purposes;

- qualification of all supervisory personnel by experience or training to carry out their supervisory responsibilities;

- required annual meeting or interview with each registered representative to discuss compliance matters relevant to his or her activities; and

- designation of registered principals to review and monitor the supervisory system.*

Though these responsibilities apply to the broker-dealer, the broker-dealer (in some cases the company) assigns them to registered principals. Some general agents and agency managers may be registered principals and be assigned supervisory responsibility. To be able to share commissions on the sale of registered products, the general agent or agency manager must at least be a registered representative of the broker-dealer.

Though states do not have a similarly explicit definition of the supervisory responsibility of a company, general agent or agency manager, in practice, they hold companies responsible for the actions of their agents. In general, the law of agency assigns the responsibility for supervision to the principal in the agent-principal relationship, typically the insurance company that has appointed the general agent or manager as its agent. Note, however, that the principal then can delegate supervisory responsibility to the general agent or manager and, although assuming responsibility for supervising the general agent or agency manager, will hold the general agent or agency manager responsible for the agent's supervision. Because of this, it is very important for the general agent or agency manager to understand clearly what responsibility the company has delegated to him or her.

---

* NASDR Conduct Rule 3010

■ HOW COMPANIES DELEGATE RESPONSIBILITY FOR SUPERVISION

For agency managers who are company employees, job descriptions, contracts and company policy and procedural statements are typical ways to define supervisory responsibilities. For general agents, contracts and company policies and procedures typically define supervisory responsibility. Both general agents and agency managers should understand fully the supervisory responsibilities assigned by the companies with which they have a relationship. Sometimes contracts and job descriptions are vague about specific supervisory duties; therefore, general agents and agency managers should pay close attention to company policies and procedural statements. Information in manuals and guidelines is often more specific about supervisory duties. General agents and agency managers who have questions about the extent of their supervisory responsibilities should ask the companies they represent for clarification.

Because one of the goals of managing compliance risk is to avoid situations that involve an inadvertent failure to supervise agents properly, the general agent and agency manager should be aware of all of a company's expectations regarding supervision. General agents and agency managers should have a detailed list of their compliance and market conduct supervisory responsibilities as a starting point in developing an effective supervisory system. Some savvy general agents and agency managers share their lists with the companies they have a relationship with to ensure that they have identified the extent of their compliance supervisory responsibilities.

General agents must be especially careful because supervisory responsibility may vary depending on the company with which the general agent has a relationship. A general agent with several company relationships needs to go beyond simply providing a list of compliance supervisory responsibilities and instead express them as a matrix that lists all of the potential supervisory responsibilities and identify which companies have assigned them. Here is an example of what one might look like:

	Company			
Compliance Responsibility	*ABC Mutual*	*XYZ Life*	*DEF Financial*	*KLM Insurance*
Review all applications for suitability	X		X	
Audit agents' files on an annual basis			X	
Review all sales involving replacements		X		X
Monitor license status semi-annually	X	X	X	X
Review and approve all requests for approval of personal sales material	X			X
Conduct mandatory compliance training for all new hires			X	
Maintain a complaint log	X	X	X	X

A matrix can help the general agent identify the extent of his or her supervisory responsibilities and provide the basis for an organized system of agent supervision. Without such a clear understanding of supervisory responsibilities, the general agent might unintentionally fail to carry them out. An example of an more complete supervisory matrix can be found in Appendix A.

A general agent or agency manager should take the following steps to identify his or her responsibilities:

- General agents or agency managers should check contracts or selling agreements, which may outline responsibilities to supervise and monitor. For example, some general agent and agency managers' contracts assign responsibility for training, which may include delivering and supervising compliance training to the general agent or agency manager.

- General agents or agency managers should ask the companies they have a relationship whether they have the responsibility for agents in their offices based on explicit or implied supervisory responsibility. For example, some companies pay agents an additional stipend for managing a detached office. General agents and agency managers need to determine whether this implies that they have supervisory responsibility for the other agents that work out of the office or whether the responsibility still falls on the general agent or agency manager.

- General agents or agency managers should get a specific description of their supervisory responsibilities from each company they have a relationship with and then make certain the description is in writing and identifies what they will be held accountable for. For example, general agents or agency managers may be responsible for reviewing the suitability of applications, maintaining appropriate agency files, reviewing correspondence, conducting audits, keeping up-to-date manuals and files, and so forth.

- General agents or agency managers should identify emergency or nonroutine types of compliance supervision, such as a regulator complaint, home office investigation, and so forth, in which the general agent or agency manager may be involved. Though these responsibilities cannot be planned for ahead of time, general agents or agency managers still should know what is expected if one of these situations occurs.

- General agents or agency managers should ask the companies they have a relationship with if they have any responsibilities for agents' administrative staff. Some contracts hold the general agent or agency manager responsible for the administrative staff in the agency.

- General agents or agency managers should collect documented procedures the general agent or agency manager is required to carry out by companies; for example, broker-dealer's requirements for conducting audits or examinations.

Appendix B, "Examples of Compliance Related Activities," contains examples of specific activities that can help develop a supervisory responsibility matrix.

■ WHY COMPANIES DELEGATE SUPERVISION

Companies delegate compliance and market conduct supervision because it is sometimes impractical to have the company's home office carry out this responsibility. Home office staff may be unable to supervise agents adequately because of the distance of the home office, the time delay in being able to take action, the lack of knowledge of details of the agent's practices, and so forth. Companies that sell through independent agents face this challenge.

The typical supervision provided by the home office is post-sale and based on exception monitoring. The home office can only begin its supervision when the application is submitted. Home offices typically have trained staff review applications to ensure that all required forms and information are provided on sales where there are potential compliance and market conduct issues. It may request additional information on applications to be able to conduct its reviews. Though it may query the agent on a particular sale, such as if an agent requests an illustration from the home office, the home office typically finds it difficult to review sales before they are submitted to it for underwriting.

Companies monitor trends and patterns in sales, complaints, agent productivity (for example, persistency) and other information (for example, client surveys) to identify potential compliance and market conduct improprieties. They look for exceptions or red flags to spot potential improprieties. For example, a company may notice that an agent has shown a dramatic increase in the number of policy lapses and that most of these policies were sold within the last two years. The company may then begin to exercise greater scrutiny of the agent's sales.

Companies provide guidelines and procedures for agents to follow and expect these procedures to be implemented and properly carried out. They may monitor this via customer surveys to determine whether clients have received information the agent is required to give them. If clients respond that they did not receive the information, the company may question that agent and impose additional requirements on any of his or her sales, for example, additional receipts and signed disclosures. Though a company may periodically review or audit the agent's operation, there are practical limitations to this.

When the company is the agent's broker-dealer, there are added requirements for regular announced and unannounced audits. Even though the NASDR accepts exception monitoring as a valid way to supervise registered representatives, exception monitoring does not replace audits and inspections.

When a general agent or agency manager is involved, the practical obstacles to direct supervision of the sale are reduced: applications can be reviewed before submission to the home office, and questions about the sale can be resolved on a timely basis. The general agent and agency manager typically are knowledgeable about the specifics of an agent's sales practices and can provide closer supervision of sales that have potential for compliance or market conduct improprieties. They can take quick action on improprieties and avoid potential compliance problems.

General agents and agency managers are better able than company home offices to conduct regular audits, inspections and reviews of agents' operations to determine that agents are following company procedures. These regular audits can help general agents and agency managers to take action on potential improprieties.

From a legal standpoint, a company wants to be able to limit its liability for improper actions taken by its agents. To do this, it should demonstrate that it provided formal, documented procedures, that audits and inspections were made, that the individuals who carried out these supervisory responsibilities were knowledgeable and that appropriate and timely actions were taken when improprieties were identified. By assigning supervisory responsibility to general agents and agency managers and providing procedures and training, the company can help limit its liability for improper actions.

POTENTIAL SUPERVISORY CHALLENGES

Conflict of Interest

There is potential conflict of interest for general agents or agency managers when dealing with the supervision of some compliance and market conduct issues. Because general agents or agency managers may be compensated in part for business produced by those agents they supervise, they potentially are under pressure to ignore errors or transgressions. General agents and agency manager should take extra care to avoid any impression that this potential conflict of interest influences their behavior.

To clear any suspicion of a conflict of interest, a general agent or agency manager should be especially careful to apply all standards equally and objectively regardless of the level of production or experience of the agents being supervised. Management action should be taken on a timely basis for all improprieties. Even the slightest impression that exceptions are made based on an agent's production or the size of a particular sale should be avoided. General agents and agency managers should take care to document that they carried out all required supervisory responsibilities so that they can defend against any allegations of this conflict of interest.

Agent's Independence

Another supervisory challenge faced by general agents and some agency managers is the agent who acts as if he or she was independent of the general agent or agency manager. Some agency managers do not face this challenge because their companies make agents submit to close supervision.

Other companies, however, assume that general agents or agency managers have greater control over agents than is realistic. Agents, especially experienced ones, may not accept supervision by general agents or agency managers. They do not want close supervision and they reject the general agent or agency manager's attempts at it. Agents may incorrectly assume that supervision of compliance and market conduct is not needed for a number of reasons:

- they believe they are ethical and that only unethical agents need supervision;

- they are experienced and equate compliance and market conduct errors with lack of sales skill or knowledge;

- they equate supervision with a lack of trust and respect;

- they feel that they have a superior level of experience and proven performance output; or

- they have not had prior problems with compliance and market conduct.

General agents and agency managers may find themselves in the difficult position of having to impose supervisory procedures on agents who will not admit that they are needed. General agents and agency managers may find themselves caught between a company that requires them to closely supervise agents and agents who resist supervision. Companies sometimes inadvertently reduce the general agent and agency manager's level of control by dealing directly with the agent.

For new agents, the general agent and agency manager must instill an acceptance of supervision of compliance and market conduct activities from the beginning of their career. Because new agents will come into contact with experienced agents who resist supervision, one must try to inoculate them against the claim that supervising compliance and market conduct is not necessary. One of the best ways to do this is to demonstrate to new agents the inherent value of supervising compliance from their first sale.

When dealing with experienced agents, general agents and agency managers can take a range of approaches to implement their supervisory responsibilities, such as:

- explaining to the agents that supervision can help them avoid potential compliance problems;

- providing agents with examples of how other agents who resisted supervision have paid a price for their resistance;

- presenting supervision as a service that can help the agent reduce their potential liability for compliance and market conduct errors;

- explaining to the agent that supervision is required by the company; or

- taking action against agents who resist supervision, such as terminating their contract.

A general agent and agency manager should not let experienced agents avoid compliance supervision. It sets a bad example for inexperienced agents and puts the experienced agent and general agent or agency manager at risk.

Delegating Responsibility

It may be unrealistic to expect a general agent or agency manager with a large staff to be involved directly in the supervision of every aspect of the agency or office. He or she must delegate some responsibilities, but the key issues to consider are which responsibilities should be delegated and what controls should be used to make sure those responsibilities are carried out properly.

Some general agents and agency managers assume that they reduce their compliance and market conduct risk by delegating responsibility for compliance and market conduct supervision. Companies use the same reasoning when they sometimes assume that they, too, reduce their risk by delegating responsibility to general agents and agency managers.

General agents or agency managers, however, may not be able to escape responsibility for supervising compliance and market conduct by delegating responsibility to someone else. This strategy actually may increase the risk that they will be held responsible for failure to supervise if they do not implement procedures and policies to monitor how delegated responsibilities are carried out.

> *For Example:* If the general agent or agency manager delegates responsibility for reviewing applications before submission to a company and does not regularly monitor that the reviews are taking place and are being done properly, he or she may be held responsible for a failure to supervise. If the individual who is given responsibility is not trained properly or is not given the resources and support needed to carry out the delegated responsibility, the general agent or agency manager also may be held responsible for a failure to properly supervise. If the general agent or agency manager allows an individual to make decisions about taking action and making exceptions without clear guidelines, the general agent and agency manager may be held responsible for those actions.

In a later section of this guide, we will discuss in greater detail the procedures and processes that general agents and agency managers can use to delegate responsibility for supervising compliance and market conduct.

Company Versus Regulators' Rules

Regulations are inconsistent between states, state regulations are sometimes inconsistent with NASDR regulations and company policies and procedures sometimes appear more strict than state or NASDR regulations. General agents and agency managers therefore are faced with the challenge of having to comply with policies and procedures that appear on the surface to be more restrictive than what regulators require. For example, a company may conduct supervisory reviews of suitability that go into greater detail or demand more documentation than the NASDR or a state requires. Because they must implement these procedures and policies, general agents and agency managers also must face the challenge of explaining to agents the company's seemingly restrictive rules.

Why Company Procedures Sometimes Are More Strict Than Regulators' Rules

Companies can choose to be more careful about compliance and market conduct than regulators and they have the right to require procedures that regulators do not. Sometimes general agents and agency managers find themselves in the difficult position of trying to explain to their agents why companies differ in their standards and procedures. Aren't they all trying to comply with the same regulations?

Companies have policies and procedures that go beyond what is required by regulators for a number of reasons. A general agent or agency manager must understand the reasons why some company policies and procedures appear more restrictive than state, federal or NASDR regulations, so that they may explain the reasoning to their agents. Following are some of those reasons:

- **Regulations may not be clear about requirements.** Many regulations offer little direction regarding procedures—they tell you what to do, but not how to do it. They describe a practice that is improper and prohibited, but fail to describe the specific procedures required to ensure that the practice does not occur. In some cases, even if the regulation contains a policy statement, it may be ambiguous, or even if it describes a specific procedure to be followed, the regulators leave it up to companies to create internal procedures to do so. Companies sometimes set standards that seem more restrictive than the regulations because they must create concrete processes and procedures where the regulators only have to outline general needs. Regulations regarding sales material and advertising provide an example. The regulators decide that words used in advertising may not misrepresent the features, benefits and cost of a product. They might even identify some words that should not be used; but they will not identify all of the potential words that could result in misrepresentation, nor will they provide guidance about the process the company should use to review sales material. As companies struggle to interpret regulations, they sometimes develop procedures or standards that appear to be more strict than the regulations in an effort to meet the regulation's intent.

- **Regulators sometimes have unwritten interpretations of standards that companies identify over time.** These interpretations then find their way into company procedures. For example, regulators who review sales materials often have additional requirements not present in their formal regulations. Comparing company procedures with the written regulations would lead someone to believe that the company's standards were more strict than the regulations, even though regulators judge based on some unwritten interpretations.

- **In large companies, several departments sometimes share responsibility for monitoring compliance.** Auditing, broker-dealer compliance, traditional product compliance, law, policyholder service, new business/underwriting and marketing departments sometimes have different perspectives on what compliance is and how it should be monitored and supervised. As each attempts to carry out its responsibility, their different perspectives and the inherent ambiguity of the regulations can lead to differences in standards, some of which may be more strict than regulators' standards.

- **States' regulations are not uniform.** Sometimes a company will develop uniform procedures or a single standard that meets every state's requirement. To do this, however, the company's standards may exceed a particular state's requirements. Having uniform company standards and procedure often is more efficient than having several. Standards offer efficiency in the programming or maintenance of computer systems, as well as in training and supervising agents. For example, some states have adopted the NAIC illustration model, while others have not. Some companies have mandated that they will follow the NAIC model in all states because it is more cost effective to have only one illustration system rather than several.

- **Terms of agreements, decrees or settlements with states or a court may require specific procedures.** Companies that have had compliance and market conduct problems in the past may have agreed to put policies and procedures in place as part of a regulator's remediation plan. Others may have had class action suits resulting in court-mandated procedures. These procedures may be more restrictive than state or NASD regulations. For example, a company may have agreed to provide a special company-developed buyer's guide to all clients as part of the agreement to settle a class action suit. They provide the guide in addition to the state-mandated guides.

- **A company may identify potential risks associated with the sale of its products and develop procedures to better manage those risks.** These procedures are designed to help the company avoid problems or provide early warnings of potential problems. Companies that have had costly class action suits may have carefully examined how to avoid such suits in the future. They would have done research to identify potential risks and how to manage them. For example, a company may find out that the complexity of one of its products requires careful disclosure by the agent and the client's signed acknowledgment. The company may require this and require field management and the home office to scrutinize applications carefully. They also may have implemented client surveys to verify client understanding of what was purchased and why.

- **A company may have failed to remove procedures when the reason is no longer valid or when they no longer serve a viable purpose.** For example, a company may have implemented a requirement that local management, a registered principal and the home office review every variable policy and contract submitted. This procedure may have been called for when these products first were sold by the company as part of its training and supervision efforts. As agents and managers became more knowledgeable about the products, only a single review by a registered principal was necessary. Multiple reviews still may occur, however, because once implemented, such procedures are hard to remove.

- **A company may belong to a self-regulatory organization that imposes higher standards than the states or the NASDR do.** For example, to be a member of the Insurance Marketplace Standards Association (IMSA), a company must have complaint-handling procedures for both verbal and written complaints. Many states require companies to have procedures for written complaints only.

- **Policies and procedures may exist for one line of business and be applied to all others.** Consistency may be driven by a desire to reinforce proper market conduct or simplify procedures. When this is done, the standards of one line of business may exceed the regulations required for others. For example, a company that uses disclosure forms for its life insurance products may implement similar forms for its property and casualty even though these forms are not required.

Limited Company Guidance

Some companies treat compliance and market conduct very seriously; others do not. Some companies may ignore state and NASDR regulations inadvertently. For example, a company may not realize that it must file advertising materials with a state or that it must respond to complaints within a specific number of business days. Other companies may believe that their policies and procedures appropriately meet minimum requirements when they do not, or that their procedures are effective when they are not. For example, a company may believe that all applications for life insurance involving replacements are reviewed to ensure that the required forms and disclosures are used. In actuality, their process may allow applications to be processed when forms are missing. Finally, some companies may not treat compliance and market conduct as seriously as they should because of a belief that the agents, and not the company, bear the responsibility for compliance.

If general agents and agency managers represent a company that provides only limited compliance and market conduct policies and procedures to serve as guidelines, then they may inadvertently allow improprieties to occur. Limited company guidance or low company standards may create compliance and market conduct risks for the general agent or agency manager.

Agency managers who are company employees typically are at less risk than the company, because they can demonstrate that they were following company procedures. However, companies that do not provide appropriate guidance still may hold the agency manager responsible for supervision under general provisions of their contract or job description to comply with all laws and regulations.

General agents appear to be at greater risk than agency managers, because their independence increases their responsibility. Because most contracts contain the provision requiring the general agent to comply with all applicable laws and regulations, the company may assume that it has less responsibility to guide or direct the general agent. The general agent who uses ignorance as a defense may find that it is not strong enough to counter his or her presumed levels of knowledge, expertise and experience.

General agents and agency managers should not solely rely on the companies they have relationships with for direction in supervising agents. A compliance-savvy general agent or agency manager should be aware of the compliance and market conduct rules and regulations that must be followed and not allow a company's low standards to put him or her at risk. A company with low compliance and market standards may prove to be a bad partner in avoiding compliance and market conduct problems.

How to Evaluate a Company's Compliance Standards

How do general agents and agency managers know if the company they have a relationship with has low compliance and market conduct standards? The following are some of the possible indicators of a company with low standards:

- The company lacks written policies and procedures regarding key compliance responsibilities; for example, there are no compliance manuals, on-line compliance guides, and so forth.

- The company provides little or no communication about compliance or market conduct related matters; for example, no updates on changes to state regulations.

- The company appears to pay little or no concern to sales involving replacements; for example, applications that are submitted without required forms are not detained in underwriting until the forms are provided.

- The company has not provided clear guidelines on how to handle customer complaints.

- The company's compliance or market conduct department has limited or no visibility; for example, there is no easily accessible way to contact them and they do not contact the general agent or agency manager.

- It is difficult to get advice and counsel from the company on compliance and market conduct issues.

- The company's chief compliance officer is not a senior executive, but a low-level manager.

- The company's sales materials (for example, brochures) often are out-of-date or lack information about important product features, benefits or conditions.

- The company's sales materials appear to have questionable assumptions or make unrealistic claims; for example, they illustrate unrealistic rates of return or project unrealistically low management and surrender fees.

- The company does not require that sales materials used by agents be approved in advance by the company.

- The company's forms, applications and procedures are so complicated that it is easy to make mistakes that can have compliance and market conduct ramifications.

- The company provides little or no training on compliance, market conduct or ethics to agents, administrative staff or managers. In addition, they do not encourage agents to build their knowledge and skills.

- The company readily makes exceptions regarding compliance and market conduct issues; for example, agents who have acted improperly are not disciplined.

- The company does not belong to the Insurance Marketplace Standards Association (IMSA).

- At company conferences, individuals who are recognized as leaders use ethically questionable sales techniques or approaches.

- The company's marketing programs encourage replacements of existing products with both their own and other companies' clients.

Contrast this with companies that have high standards. The following are some of the possible indicators that a company has high standards:

- **The company provides regular updates on compliance issues of interest to the general agent, agency manager and agent.** It provides regular educational information on practical aspects of compliance in a straightforward format, such as a newsletter, that makes it easy for general agents, agency managers or agents to refresh their knowledge and understanding of compliance rules and regulations.

- **The company encourages the agent to develop general knowledge and skills by providing training materials and opportunities.** The more the agent knows about products, systems, marketing, and so forth, the more likely he or she will avoid creating compliance problems through unintentional errors. Good compliance support includes helping the agent keep marketing and sales skills sharp using written materials, training sessions or individual coaching by company representatives.

- **The company helps the agent identify potential compliance problems in his or her practice.** A company with high standards provides material and services that help the agent self-supervise, and its supervisory support is meant to help the agent avoid potential compliance problems in his or her business or practice. This includes helping the agent educate and supervise associates and administrative staff, providing questionnaires and checklists the agent can use to identify ways to avoid compliance violations and conducting company or third-party audits and examinations.

- **The company helps the general agent or agency manager supervise the agent's practice.** A company with high standards provides tools and materials to the general agent or agency manager.

- **The company has a reputation of standing behind their general agents, agency managers and agents when compliance questions arise.** It sees itself as a partner in doing the right thing by the client. Market conduct and compliance are a part of its normal way of doing business, and it believes it should share responsibility for the market conduct of its agents. This is one of the reasons why it takes pains to support the compliance and market conduct efforts of its general agents, agency managers and agents.

How can you tell if a company meets these criteria? First, look to see if it is a member of the IMSA. A company that is a member of IMSA has demonstrated that it treats compliance as a priority and is willing to support good market conduct. Next, ask the company to provide you with a copy of its compliance policies and procedures, inquire about its policy regarding sales material review and ask for copies of its educational material on compliance. Talk to the company's compliance staff as well as other general agents or agency managers who have had a relationship with the company about the support it provides.

Next time you are thinking about a relationship with a new company or one you currently represent, compliance support should be added to the list of criteria you use to make the choice. In the long run, it may save you from ending up as a co-defendant in court.

3

Developing an Effective Compliance and Market Conduct Supervisory System

GENERAL CHARACTERISTICS OF AN EFFECTIVE COMPLIANCE AND MARKET CONDUCT SUPERVISORY SYSTEM

Every general agent and agency manager should have an effective compliance and market conduct supervisory system to control compliance and market conduct risk. For some, this system has been provided by the companies with which they have relationships; others have developed their own systems through trail and error. Some do not have an effective system, but at best only some procedures they carry out periodically.

The following are the general characteristics of an effective system:

- **Efficiency.** Whatever system the general agent or agency manager uses, it must be simple, straightforward and efficient. A difficult supervisory system will either not be used or be used incorrectly.

- **Trust.** The supervisory system must be based on trust in the agent, administrative staff and management. Without this trust the system will fail because no system can be expected to identify every potential market conduct issue. Such a system would need to be too intrusive into the sales process, agent practices and manager operations. A supervisory system can only control risk; it cannot eliminate it.

- **Integration into normal operations.** A supervisory system must make compliance part of every process in the agency or office. If it is extraneous to routine activities, it will not be effective. Compliance and market conduct should be part of everyone's everyday job in an agency or office, as should supervisory systems.

- **Proper implementation and maintenance.** New supervisory systems or changes to current procedures must be implemented properly to minimize the potential for resistance from agents and administrative staff, which can undermine the effectiveness of any supervisory system. Agents and administrative staff need to be shown how the system benefits them—such training is key to effectively implementing a new system or changing an existing system. Once implemented, a supervisory system needs to be updated, modified and fine tuned as products, markets, and relationships with companies change. These changes should not be made without concern for their effect on agents, administrative staff and management.

- **Tailored to the agency or office.** An important characteristic of an effective supervisory system is that it is tailored to the needs and circumstances of the agency or office where it is used. Because each general agent or agency manager runs their agency differently, there is no one compliance and market conduct supervisory system that all should or could use. Each general agent or agency manager should develop his or her own system or modify the systems that are mandated by the companies which with he or she has a relationship.

■ KEY ELEMENTS OF AN EFFECTIVE COMPLIANCE AND MARKET CONDUCT SUPERVISORY SYSTEM

The following are the key elements of an effective compliance and market conduct supervisory system:

- explicit standards of conduct;

- clear policies and procedures for agents and administrative staff;

- communication and implementation of policies and procedures;

- regular monitoring and supervision of conduct;

- timely and appropriate actions to resolve improper conduct; and

- integration of compliance and market conduct into normal operations.

In the following sections of this guide we will provide details about each of these elements. The first three will be covered in Chapter 4, "Developing and Communicating Explicit Standards of Conduct." Chapter 5, "Monitoring and Supervising Compliance and Market Conduct," will cover the next two elements—monitoring and taking action. Chapter 7, "How to Integrate Compliance and Market Conduct into Managing for Success," will cover the final element.

Though some agents may accept the need for rules and regulations, others will be critical of the way companies react to state and NASDR rules and regulations. They may feel frustrated by a company's policies and procedures and see them as barriers to effective selling. Some agents believe their jobs are difficult enough without the added burden of incomprehensible rules and regulations that seem not to apply to them. In addition, success as an agent tends to be related to an independent, entrepreneurial spirit, a characteristic often at odds with the discipline and restrictions imposed by systems for supervising compliance and market conduct.

> **ILL. 3.1 ■ *Using a Company-Mandated Supervisory System***
>
> Some agency managers and general agents are required to use a company-mandated system for supervision. The NASDR requires that a broker-dealer have a supervisory system, and this is the one companies most often mandate for use by their general agents or agency managers. Some companies require their general agents or agency managers to use a mandated supervisory system that includes both registered and nonregistered products.
>
> Even when the general agent or agency manager must use a mandated supervisory system, it is important to tailor it so that it is efficient and effective in that particular agency. This can sometimes present challenges because companies can be inflexible about making changes to their mandated supervisory systems. General agents and agency managers who are required to use a specific supervisory system should discuss possible modifications with the company that mandated the system.

Because most agents are ethical people who do not need to be closely supervised and controlled, compliance functions in companies are often the target of agent animosity. They sometimes are jokingly referred to as the "sales prevention department." Much agent dissatisfaction with aggressively enforced compliance policies and procedures may stem from their ignorance of corporate responsibility for the actions of agents appointed to sell their products.

The general agent and agency manager sometimes find themselves in the middle of a difficult situation because they must carry out a company's supervisory requirements against the wishes of their agents and administrative staffs. The process discussed in this book can go a long way to making the supervisory responsibilities of the general agent and agency manager understandable and palatable to agents and administrative staff.

4

Developing and Communicating Explicit Standards of Conduct

■ WHAT ARE EXPLICIT STANDARDS OF CONDUCT?

Explicit standards of conduct often are documented in a formal, written statement of the conduct expected of everyone in the agency, office or company. These statements are sometimes called *codes of conduct, ethics statements, business practices codes, company statements of policy* or *principles.* Sometimes they are included in company mission statements, in company manuals or training materials or in separate documents.

They typically cover a wide range of issues at a fairly high level of generalization. For example, they may set a standard that all sales be suitable to the client and based on a documented needs analysis. The typical standard of conduct statement often does not go into detail about the specific aspects of suitability that should be taken into account or the needs analysis procedure that should be used. These details are critical, but they are more effectively communicated in the agent's, offices' or company's documented policies and procedures that are contained in manuals, guides or on-line information databases.

Because the standards of conduct do not contain the details necessary to apply, use or supervise the standards, they do not replace the need for detailed policies and procedures.

■ WHY ARE EXPLICIT STANDARDS OF CONDUCT NEEDED?

Explicit standards of conduct foster correct attitudes among agents, administrative staff and management and demonstrate a commitment to proper compliance and market conduct. Because they are documented, they are a useful tool for communicating and educating people and serve as evidence that standards do exist. Disciplining individuals who do not live up to the written standards demonstrates that they are expected to be followed. This, in turn, demonstrates that the agency takes compliance and market conduct seriously, which reduces compliance and market conduct risk.

> **ILL. 4.1 ▪ *The Heart of the Matter***
>
> When beginning the process of developing an office statement or code, some general agents and agency managers find it valuable to step back and think about their business and what they stand for. Most general agents and agency managers focus their time, energy and commitment on building relationships and sales. This investment often is motivated by an underlying set of principles and beliefs that, for many, are more important than financial gain. For example, a commitment to customer service leads many general agents and agency managers to invest in talent and technology to run their back office or to terminate a relationship with a producer who has failed to provide clients with proper service. For some general agents and agency managers, integrity is not something that they need to be successful, it is a part of their core beliefs, principles and values—something the general agent's or agency manager's statement or code should reflect.

Some general agents and agency managers feel that explicit standards of conduct are superfluous, because there are detailed standards in extensive policy and procedure guides and manuals. However, a formal written code of conduct is a valuable way to provide a comprehensive picture of expectations for staff. The details of what must be done and how it should be done can obscure the basic concept of what is expected.

Each agency should have one set of standards. This might not present a problem for agency managers with a primary company relationship because their company may mandate that they use that company's statement; but for general agents with a number of company relationships it can be problematic. The statements most likely will disagree with one another and may have different approaches to key issues, such as replacements. Having many standards in an agency or office can create confusion and decrease the strength and value of a set of explicit standards.

Agency managers with a company-mandated set of standards still may want to develop their own set, because some companies' standards are not well defined.

■ HOW TO DEVELOP AN AGENCY OR OFFICE STATEMENT OR CODE

A general agent or agency manager may find it helpful to review the statements of companies he or she has relationships with when developing his or her own. These statements should be analyzed to identify the issues or topics they cover. Before finalizing any agency or office statement, the general agent or agency manager should ensure that his or her agency or office statement covers all of the issues raised in the statements of the companies he or she represents. Leaving one out may create the appearance that the issue is not important.

Choosing to use one company's standards of conduct statement can be unwise if the company chosen has lenient compliance or market conduct standards. The lower an agency's compliance and market conduct standards, the greater the risk that associates will think low standards are acceptable.

The general agent or agency manager should next identify the key issues and topics that apply to the markets and products his or her agents face. For additional information, general agents and agency managers can use the statements or codes of an industry association statement of conduct (e.g., the Society of Financial Service Professionals or the Insurance Marketplace Standards Association). A manager may choose the statements that apply and edit them to fit his or her agency or office.

The general agent or agency manager may find it valuable to involve agents and their staff in the process of developing the standards. They will have greater ownership in standards—and they are more likely to follow them—if they have been invited to participate in tailoring them to the agency or office.

Some agency or office statements will be several pages long to cover a wide range of issues. The following are some of the key issues that should be addressed in the statement:

- customer service;
- complaint handling and dispute resolution;
- replacements;
- suitability;
- education and training;
- disclosure and client education;
- confidentiality and privacy;
- underwriting and insurability; and
- representations, advertising, sales materials and illustrations.

An agency or office statement also should refer the agent to any statements or codes of conduct specific to the companies he or she represents.

Some general agents and agency managers also include in their statements of conduct standards for subjects such as equal opportunity, workplace harassment, and so forth.

You can find a sample standards of conduct statement in Appendix C.

HOW TO COMMUNICATE STANDARDS OF CONDUCT

Having a standards of conduct statement is useless unless it is communicated effectively. The most important element in communicating standards of conduct is for the general agent or agency manager to make it clear that he or she is fully committed to the standards. The agents and administrative staff must believe that the standards will be enforced. If the general agent or agency manager appears uncommitted or to be merely paying lip service to the standards, it will have a negative impact on the compliance and market conduct of the agents and administrative staff.

Agency staff may perceive the lack of full support and belief in the standards as a tacit acknowledgment that compliance and market conduct are not critical and that failure to act properly will be condoned.

Each general agent and agency manager should analyze his or her attitude toward compliance and market conduct carefully. Nothing will speak louder than their actions and beliefs. The general agent or agency manager's behavior determines whether his or her associates take compliance and market conduct seriously. To gain insight into your own commitment to compliance and market conduct, see the information presented in Appendix D, "The Concept of Ethical Leadership."

Some general agents and agency managers conduct an implementation meeting to introduce the standards statement. The general agent or agency manager makes a presentation based on the statement that demonstrates full support for it and the commitment to monitor conduct and take action against those agents and administrative staff who fail to live up to the standards.

General agents and agency managers also should discuss with staff how they benefit from following the standards. No one wants to work for an organization that has a bad local reputation or in an environment that is being investigated and examined for potential improprieties. No one likes to work with clients with whom relationships are strained or antagonistic because of improper conduct. The long-term overall success of an agency or office and the people who work there is directly related to the quality of the service provided to clients, and compliance and market conduct are key elements in the quality service equation.

Everyone in the agency or office should get a copy of the standards of conduct statement. Many general agents and agency managers require everyone who receives a copy of the standards statement to sign a form acknowledging that they have read, understood and will abide by it. This is another way to communicate the fact that the standards are serious business. The general agent or agency manager then files the acknowledgment so that if anyone does not live up to the standards, he or she cannot claim ignorance of them.

In addition to the initial implementation meeting, many general agents and agency managers follow-up by posting the standards in a prominent place in the agency.

The agency standards of conduct statement should be used when recruiting agents, administrative staff and managers. All new hires should receive a copy and sign the acknowledgment form. The standards of conduct statement should be included in new employee training and education programs to reinforce its importance.

Relevant parts of the standards of conduct statement should be reviewed at agency meetings to demonstrate their importance. For example, at an agency meeting where new replacement procedures are discussed, the general agent or agency manager can begin by mentioning that replacements are part of the agency or office standards of conduct statement.

■ CLEAR POLICIES AND PROCEDURES

To have an effective compliance and market conduct supervisory system, everyone in the agency or office must know the compliance and market conduct policies and procedures of the companies with which they have a relationship. Current versions of those policies and procedures should be readily available so that they can read and follow them. Some companies and broker-dealers require their agents or registered representatives to maintain file of current company policies and procedures.

For an agency manager with only one company relationship, the challenge of obtaining and maintaining clear compliance and market conduct policies and procedures is much more manageable than for a general agent with several company relationships. For general agents or managers who have relationships with several companies, the task of obtaining and maintaining policies and procedures increases the need for a process for maintaining up-to-date and organized information.

WHAT INFORMATION DO AGENTS AND ADMINISTRATIVE STAFF NEED?

A master file of compliance and market conduct information should be maintained and available. It should include at least the following:

- specific compliance and market conduct policies and procedures of the agency or office;

- specific compliance and market conduct procedures of all of the companies with which the agents in the agency or office have relationships;

- general company standards as described in ethics or conduct statements;

- updates, changes and enhancements to policies and procedures;

- administrative procedures of the companies with which agents in the agency or office have relationships;

- all communications from companies on compliance and market conduct;

- all training programs on compliance and market conduct used by the agency or office; and

- general reference books on compliance and market conduct.

Administrative procedures are required because administrative errors often lead to compliance problems. Updates of agency or office and company policies are needed to provide agents and administrative staff with the most current information as well as a basis for determining when changes should take effect. State regulations for all states in which agents conduct business and NASDR regulations also should be provided to serve as a reference when questions arise.

It is sometimes thought that agents and administrative staff need different information resources, but it is best if both agents and administrative have the same information. In this way, each can gain an appreciation of the role the other plays in helping ensure proper compliance and market conduct by knowing the policies and procedures they must work with.

HOW TO MAKE POLICIES AND PROCEDURES CLEAR

Policies and procedures sometimes are not as clear as they could be. What seems straightforward to the home office can be confusing to agents and administrative staff, or a specific policy or procedure may be difficult to find in manuals or guides. For policies and procedures to be effective, the users must be able to understand them.

To avoid misinterpretation of requirements and procedures, some general agents and agency managers provide the following:

- summaries of key compliance and market conduct policies and procedures;

- references to the location of specific information in manuals and guides;

- examples of correctly and incorrectly completed forms, such as replacement forms;

- checklists of key steps that must be followed to carry out a procedure properly;

- the names of individuals in the agency or office who have mastered the procedure and can provide advice; and

- the names of individuals at companies who can answer questions.

The information that needs to be summarized for agents and administrative staff depends on the complexity of the policy or procedure and the compliance risk involved. Summaries, examples and checklists developed by agents, administrative staff, general agents or agency managers always should be reviewed by the company whose policy or procedures are being clarified to ensure their accuracy.

There are several ways to identify areas in which agents and administrative staff may need summary or clarification. Problems with underwriting, such as returned applications, questions from a home office compliance department or potential improprieties identified by an audit, may signal unclear policies and procedures. Agents and their administrative staff can be surveyed to identify policies and procedures that raise questions or create problems.

HOW TO MAINTAIN COMPLIANCE AND MARKET CONDUCT POLICIES AND PROCEDURES

Responsibility for creating and maintaining a master file of all information related to compliance and market conduct should be delegated to one person. The assignment of this responsibility and a description of the duties it entails should be documented in either a job description or memorandum to file. This documentation should be kept in the general agent or agency manager's compliance and market conduct file.

The person responsible for the master file should collect and organize the most up-to-date copy of all company manuals, guides and other materials, thereby creating the master file. If there has never been an agency or office master file it often is best

> **ILL. 4.2 ■ *Creating a Compliance Tip File***
>
> A compliance tip file is a list of names, titles and telephone numbers that includes the area of expertise of the person at the companies with which agents have a relationship.
>
> For example, one may ask, what is the most up-to-date sales material for a specific product? What forms are needed for an internal replacement of an annuity in a particular state? By providing a list of the right person to call for a particular issue, questions about policies and procedures can be answered more easily. If they have an easier time finding an answer to their questions and resolutions to their problems, agents and administrative staff are less likely to perceive compliance as a burden.
>
> By being able to call the right person on the first attempt, agents and administrative staff will save time and be more likely to get the right answer to their questions. The problem of getting correct information easily can be magnified if agents and administrative staff have relationships with several companies or if a company has several areas (for example, corporate, regional, zone, and so forth) that deal with compliance.
>
> General agents, agency managers and administrative staff typically can learn through experience to identify the right person to call. A general agent or agency manager can develop an agency or office tip file by asking a company to identify whom to call with questions and their area of expertise. These names then should be tested to determine whether they are correct. The list may also include the names of agents and administrative staff who understand compliance well and can be counted on to provide practical advice.

not to rely on the current versions of company manuals available in the office. The most up-to-date versions should be obtained.

The general agent or agency manager should contact the companies his or her agents have relationships with and ask them to send all changes and updates to that one person. Others in the agency and office should know that this person is responsible for the master file so that they obtain any information they may need. The general agent or agency manager also should provide that person with any information he or she receives.

Some agencies and offices seem to have an endless supply of updates, notes, new procedures, manuals, and so forth on compliance and market conduct. Keeping track of all this information and keeping the agency or office master file up-to-date is a challenge. If the agency or office does business with several companies, the effort it takes to organize and keep track of compliance communications multiplies.

A log or listing of all of the updates and changes that are communicated is a key tool for supervising the maintenance of policies and procedures. The log should contain the date the updates were received, the source and the date the agency or office information was updated. The person responsible for maintaining the agency or office's compliance and market conduct master file should maintain the log. The maintenance of the companies' policies and procedures should be monitored regularly. The general agent or agency manager should periodically check the log and determine that changes have been made to the master file on a timely basis.

Tips on Maintaining the Master File

It is important to realize that, once created, maintaining the master file is not a difficult task.

After logging the information, the first step is to highlight when it takes effect. This should be noted in the log. If it is an e-mail message, print it out. If it is a manual with a cover note or transmittal note, the note should be saved with the manual.

If the information signals a significant change in policies and procedures and it takes effect within the next 30 days, disseminate it immediately. Often the message is not that urgent. Everything other than urgent communications can be filed in a new compliance updates file. This can be anything—a folder, box, drawer, etc.—as long as it is someplace where this information will not get misplaced or lost before it can be dealt with.

Every month, the person responsible for the master file should go to the updates file and organize the contents. If your agents have relationships with more than one company, the next step is to sort the information and communications by company. For each company, the agency or office should have a chronological compliance file of updates and communications. A ring binder is a good place for this.

The person responsible for the master file should take the new communications and review the compliance file to determine their implications. It often is a good idea to organize each company's chronological file by subject to allow quick access to information. The easiest way to do this is to use a different colored flag; for example, blue for replacements, red for underwriting, green for correspondence, and so forth. If the communication is a duplicate, which often happens, it will be clear because the documents will appear together. It is a good idea, however, not to throw duplicates out. They should be filed, but only the most up-to-date procedures should have colored flags. This cuts down on the number of flags and makes it easier to find current procedures. If the communication is too large to be put into a ring binder, such as a manual would be, put a page in the binder that identifies the information and where it is in the agency or office. The cover note that came with the manual or a copy of its cover often is used.

With a master file in place, people will know where to go for the information when a question arises. The most recent policy statement should be easy to identify, and there is less likelihood that important communications or updates will be missed.

Only one agency or office master file should exist. It should be kept in one place so that it can be maintained easily and protected. Some agencies or offices set aside a filing cabinet or a bookshelf in the general agent's administrative area for the master file. The use of the master file should be supervised to ensure people do not remove pages or materials from it.

It is best if the file is organized by company and by topic within company. Labels, separate files and other devices should be used to identify each company's policies and materials clearly. Brightly colored labels are a good way to highlight policies and procedures for replacements, complaint handling, licensing, suitability and other important topics. Some agencies or offices use a separate file drawer for each company's information and keep different manuals, guides, updates, etc., in different folders.

Each agent should keep a compliance and market conduct reference library available to administrative staff in his or her office. From a practical perspective, the master file may not always be accessible when an agent needs it. For example, an agent may be working on a case at night after the general agent or agency manager's office is closed. The agent's compliance and market conduct reference library should contain all of the information in the master file. However, agents should tailor their files to highlight the information they need on a regular basis. For example, if an agent predominantly sells one company's products, he or she likely will refer to that company's policies and procedures more often and will want to have them handy.

Agents and administrative staff should know that the master file exists and how it can be used. They should understand that each company's specific policy and procedures must be followed when dealing with their products. Use of the master file should be a part of every new employee's training.

COMMUNICATION AND IMPLEMENTATION OF POLICIES AND PROCEDURES

Being in compliance means paying attention to details when working with policies, rules, procedures. It takes organization and follow-through to be in compliance with state and NASDR rules and regulations and company policies and procedures. Not only must agents and their administrative staff keep their compliance and market conduct reference file up-to-date, they also must keep their knowledge of what is in those files current. This means that agents and administrative staff need ongoing communication, education and training on compliance and market conduct.

How to Educate Agents and Administrative Staff About the Importance of Compliance and Market Conduct

Action is the best way to communicate the importance of compliance and market conduct. Agents and administrative staff will know that compliance and market conduct are important if they observe the general agent or agency manager following through on the agency or office's standards of conduct. The general agent and agency manager should review the information in Appendix D, "The Concept of Ethical Leadership," to see how to demonstrate the importance of compliance and market conduct.

Educating new employees begins when they are recruited. Early in the recruitment process, the general agent or agency manger should show them the agency or office statement of conduct and explain why it is important. The new recruit must know that every employee is required to live up to the standards of conduct.

Both new and current agents need to understand why proper compliance and market conduct is in their best interest. To do this they need to understand the negative impact of improper conduct. Appendix E, "Being Out of Compliance Is Bad for

> **ILL. 4.3 ■ *The Right Balance***
>
> When selecting agents and administrative staff, you should evaluate the person's prior experiences with their attitude toward compliance and market conduct. Integrating compliance and market conduct into the selection process will be covered in Chapter 7. During the appointment process, companies sometimes require the agent to acknowledge receipt of a company statement of ethics or conduct. Rather than treating this as just another piece of paperwork needed by a company to process an appointment, the general agent or agency manager should use it as an opportunity to reinforce the importance of compliance and market conduct.

Business—An Agent's Perspective," identifies the negative consequences of becoming involved in cases of improper compliance and market conduct. The information in Appendix D should be tailored for the type of employee and used to increase awareness of the importance of proper market conduct.

General agents and agency managers sometimes fail to pay attention to the differences between agents' practices, markets and personalities when considering how to increase their awareness to compliance and market conduct. Some markets have higher levels of compliance risk, for example, sales to seniors. Agents who work in these markets may need to be more aware of compliance policies and procedures and vigilant in the efforts to avoid potential compliance issues.

Some agents are less sensitive to the importance of details. Some have a natural tendency to resist following rules, regulations and procedures. These agents need to be made aware of the necessity of following company policies and procedures. General agents and agency managers should pay attention to those agents who need more education on the importance of compliance and market conduct.

General agents and agency managers should regularly communicate to their agents and administrative staff that compliance and market conduct and company policies and procedures are important. Sometimes experienced agents and administrative staff become complacent about compliance and market conduct because they worked through the mid to late 1990s, when compliance and market conduct training and education were emphasized. Regardless of experience, all agents and administrative staff need continuing training to reinforce and update their knowledge. The experienced agent or administrative staff member must be reminded of the importance of compliance and market conduct so that he or she will be more willing to continue their education on the subject.

Compliance-savvy general agents and agency managers know that the message of the importance of compliance and market conduct must be repeated. They find ways to get this message across in meetings, bulletins, new product implementations, performance reviews and coaching and counseling sessions.

How to Overcome Negative Reactions to Compliance and Market Conduct

Negative reactions are common when general agents and agency managers communicate standards, policies, procedures, programs and general information. Methods to overcome a negative reaction depend on its cause.

- **Lack of understanding and fear of the unknown.** In some cases, the negative reaction is caused by ignorance or fear. Often, the more agents and administrative staff know about what the agency manager and agency supervisor plan to do and why, the easier it will be for them to adapt to the enhancements in standards, policies, procedures and processes.

- **Lack of perceived need for guidance.** Agents and administrative staff, especially experienced ones, often do not believe they need standards, policies and procedures to be in compliance and to avoid improper market conduct. Because they do not understand the need, they are not interested in the message. These agents and administrative staff must understand how easy it is to make an inadvertent compliance or market conduct error. They will benefit from learning about how even experienced, highly ethical agents have created problems for themselves through inadvertent errors.

- **Failure to understand the benefits.** Some agents and administrative staff do not understand how compliance and market conduct standards, policies and procedures actually benefit them. They see these controls, rules and regulations only as more work. These agents and administrative staff must better understand the costs of improper conduct.

  It can be important to point out the value of knowing the standards, policies and regulations that agents and administrative staff must follow to avoid problems. Agents may dislike the complications caused by the income, business and estate tax regulations, but they accept that they must follow those rules. Compliance and market conduct standards, policies and procedures are no different from tax laws. Agents and administrative staff must better understand this similarity.

- **Compliance is extra work.** Some agents and administrative staff are negative because of the extra work compliance creates. Most likely they are reacting to the confusion and complexity of standards, policies and procedures. These agents and administrative staff must find ways of integrating them into their normal practices seamlessly so that they are not such a hindrance. Involving agents in their design, development and implementation can lessen the potential negative impact on workflow.

The easier the standards, policies and procedures are to implement the more likely they will be accepted. Get agents, administrative staff and other managers involved in making them as easy to follow as possible. Their involvement will improve the final system and ensure that they have ownership in the process. Be sure that any systems work effectively and efficiently before implementing them on a widespread basis. Pilot test and refine them before implementing them throughout agency or office.

It is also important to note that not everyone has a negative reaction to standards, policies and procedures. Sometimes having one or two agents with positive attitudes toward compliance and market conduct test the procedures first can help identify potential issues with the procedures while creating some support for them among other agents.

What Role Does Compliance and Market Conduct Training Play in a Supervisory System?

Knowledge is power in the area of compliance and market conduct particularly for the general agent and agency manager. To provide proper supervision, a general agent or agency manager must know the rules so he or she can apply and explain them to agents and administrative staff. The general agent or agency manager need not be an expert in every rule and procedure, but must know enough to coach, counsel and train others. In addition, if the general agent or agency manager demonstrates knowledge of the rules, it sets a good example to the others in the agency or office. A good supervisor is a good teacher, and a good teacher must know the subject matter.

General agents and agency managers should begin developing compliance and market conduct training by collecting the information and training materials provided by the companies with which they have a relationship. They should study them to build skills and knowledge as well as to identify the resources available to build their own training program.

Knowledge of compliance and market conduct means more than knowing what the rules and regulations are—how to apply those rules and regulations in every day situations is equally important. The goal of any formal compliance training should be to reduce compliance risk. To do this, training should be practical and applied. It should focus on general principals of compliance and market conduct as well as on the specifics of products and procedures. Agents and administrative staff often come away from training loaded down with specific requirements and only a vague idea of how to apply them to their jobs.

In many cases, general agents or agency managers don't have to develop compliance and market conduct training materials because companies provide training on these subject. Some provide complete training programs; others may provide only reference materials. A general agent or agency manager should review available training materials, evaluate the practicality of the training and then organize it all into a practical curriculum. Most general agents and agency managers can fashion a complete compliance and market conduct training program from the materials provided by various companies.

The training program should be documented, and the general agent or agency manager should keep a copy in the compliance and market conduct files. The curriculum documentation should include:

- materials to be used;

- attendees;

- schedule of sessions;

- testing done to measure comprehension of the material; and
- train-the-trainer sessions held to prepare for the program.

This training program and the materials to be used should be filed with the attendance lists from the various sessions. Some companies require this information to be kept, but even if they do not, it is valuable evidence that this aspect of proper supervision was carried out.

Some companies mandate that all agents, administrative staff and managers attend compliance, market conduct or ethics training. The general agent or agency manager should follow company procedures to ensure that this training takes place as recommended by the company. However, a general agent or agency manager may want to evaluate whether the company-mandated training provides sufficient coverage of compliance and market conduct issues and whether it is practical and applied enough to help reduce compliance risk. Sometimes, company-provided training does not cover all the issues facing an agent or administrative staff member. Relying on this training could provide a false sense of security. Agents and administrative staff might think they are knowledgeable enough to avoid potential compliance and market conduct problem, when they really are not. This training often can be integrated into the overall curriculum.

To ensure that the training program is complete and appropriate, the general agent or agency manager can ask companies with which he or she has relationships to review the program.

Agents and administrative staff should receive compliance training and education, regardless of how much experience they have. The program should provide training tailored to the needs of both new and experienced associates. State and NASDR requirements for continuing education should not be relied on to fully meet every agent's needs.

Sometimes a general agent or agency manager whose agents have relationships with several companies is faced with having an array of company-mandated compliance programs to implement. It is sometimes impractical to have agents and administrative staff participate in several programs dealing with the topic of compliance and market conduct. This is another reason why a general agent or agency manager may want to develop his or her own compliance training program built on the resources provided by several companies.

New agent and administrative staff training should include compliance and market conduct in a prominent position. These subjects should never appear as an afterthought or add on. In Chapter 7 we will provide more ideas on how to make training on compliance and market conduct effective.

How to Keep People Up-to-Date on Policies and Procedures

As policies, procedures and regulations change, the general agent or agency manager should make certain that the agents and administrative staff are made aware of the changes. A procedure for keeping everyone in the agency or office up to date is needed.

The best way to do this is to assign responsibility for communicating changes to the person who is responsible for maintaining the master file of policies and procedures. This person should be the nexus of all information on changes. He or she should regularly communicate the changes to policies, procedures and regulations to everyone in the agency. Often there are several notifications of changes from various sources. By having one person in the agency responsible for coordinating the communication of all changes, the confusion caused by duplicate notifications can be reduced.

Communication about changes should be easily recognized. For example, some agencies or offices have a brightly colored cover sheet for the changes. Some agencies or offices stamp all compliance-related information with the word *compliance* in bold, red letters. Some agencies or offices put *Compliance-Important* in the subject line of all e-mails that deal with the subject. Other agencies or offices send out notices of changes on their intranets.

Another useful technique is to send out notices of any changes at a specific time each week or month, such as every other Monday. Specific changes to company policies and procedures or regulations then are attached to a recognizable cover page. The notice outlines the changes and when they become effective, describes their importance or impact and provides instructions on how to implement them. Because the person responsible for the master file should already have reviewed how to implement the changes, his or her advice can facilitate the task others face in implementing the change. By creating a system that regularly communicates changes, the agency or office comes to expect the communication and learns how to use it effectively.

Sometimes the communication requires agents and administrative staff to update their reference libraries on compliance and market conduct by removing pages from company policy guides and manuals and replacing them with new ones. For companies that have their polices and procedures on their web site or on computer infobases, the notice alerts the agents and administrative staff to review the changes to learn their impact.

Having one person as the nexus for communicating changes provides a resource for everyone in the agency if questions arise.

Copies of the notices should be maintained in the master file to serve as documentation that the changes have been communicated. Agents and administrative staff should maintain copies of the notices in their files as evidence that they received them. When examinations or audits are done, a review of the files will help identify if the process of communicating changes is being done effectively in the agency or office.

5
Monitoring and Supervising Compliance and Market Conduct

Many general agents and agency managers rely on their observations and interactions with agents and administrative staff as a basis for identifying potential issues. For a small agency or office this may be effective, however, most general agents and agency managers need an early warning system for spotting potential market conduct and compliance problems.

Smoke detectors in our homes and offices are effective because they alert us to a potential fire while it is still small and there is just a little smoke in the air. This gives us time to put out the fire or take precautions, to escape the danger. General agents and agency managers need the same kind of early warning system for compliance problems.

■ WHY ARE MONITORING AND SUPERVISING COMPLIANCE AND MARKET CONDUCT IMPORTANT?

The primary purpose of monitoring and supervising compliance and market conduct is to identify and address potential problems. Once identified, these potential problems can be resolved expeditiously, thereby avoiding the need for serious disciplinary actions. Monitoring and supervision are also good ways to identify the training needs of agents and administrative staff. This training and education often can become part of the general agent or agency manager's normal counseling and coaching. Finally, by providing ongoing monitoring and supervision, the general agent or agency manager demonstrates proactive concern for proper compliance and market conduct—such activities may protect them from accusations that they failed to supervise the agents and administrative staff.

■ HOW TO ASSESS CURRENT MONITORING AND SUPERVISION SYSTEMS

Most general agents and agency managers already do some monitoring and supervision of compliance and market conduct. The monitoring and supervision system outlined in this section can serve as a basis for identifying enhancements to the general agent or agency manager's current activities.

1. The general agent or agency manager should begin by identifying his or her responsibilities for monitoring and supervision. Refer to the discussion in Chapter 2 of the need for a general agent or agency manager to develop a responsibility matrix, as well as the list of examples of compliance and market conduct responsibilities in Chapter 1. An example of the type of matrix we suggest general agents and agency managers create is presented in Appendix A.

   The following activities may also prove helpful in accomplishing this step:

   - Check contracts or selling agreements, which may outline responsibilities that carry with them the need to supervise and monitor. For example, some general agent and agency managers' contracts assign them responsibility for training, which may include delivering and supervising compliance training.

   - Ask the companies one has a relationship with whether responsibility for agents is explicit or implied. For example, some companies pay agents an additional stipend for managing a detached office. Does this imply that these agents have supervisory responsibility for the other agents that work out of the office or does the responsibility still fall to the general agent or agency managers?

   - Get a specific description of supervisory responsibilities from each company. Make sure it is in writing and identifies what the general agent or agency manager will be held accountable for, for example, reviewing the suitability of applications, maintaining appropriate agency files, reviewing correspondence, conducting audits, keeping up-to-date manuals and files, and so forth.

   - Identify emergency or nonroutine types of compliance supervision. The general agent or agency manager may be involved in a regulator complaint or home office investigation. Though the exact details of these responsibilities cannot be known in advance, the general agent or agency manager still should know what will be expected of him or her.

   - Ask companies about responsibilities for agents' administrative staff. Some contracts hold the general agent or agency manager responsible for the administrative staff in the agency.

   - Collect documented procedures. The general agent or agency manager must collect documented procedures required by the companies he or she represents, for example, broker-dealer's requirements for conducting audits or examinations.

   In addition, the general agent or agency manager should identify the following:

   - market conduct and compliance risks that are more prevalent in the markets in which his or her agents work, for example, sales to seniors, cross selling of life insurance and property and casualty products, replacements, selling in several jurisdictions, etc.;

- results of any independent audits or examinations for potential monitoring and supervisory issues or needs; and

- supervisory responsibilities that have been delegated to second-line managers or administrative staff.

2. Next, the general agent or agency manager should identify the information currently used to carry out the responsibilities listed, their setting and their timing by doing the following:

- Identify the compliance reports, for example, reports of specific compliance or market conduct activities, such as replacements or applications rejected or delayed because of suitability questions.

- Identify information that must be maintained or documented, for example, forms, checklists, and so forth, used to document or accomplish the responsibilities, such as application review checklists or replacement red flag checklists.

- Collect examples of reports received that are related to compliance and market conduct, for example, performance or productivity reports or persistency reports.

- Identify the venues or settings used to monitor and supervise, for example, performance or productivity meetings, annual planning sessions or annual compliance meetings.

- Identify the normal frequency of supervisory meetings with agents.

This information should be included in the matrix.

3. Once all this information has been identified, the general agent or agency manager should reorganize the matrix by doing the following:

- Create a column in the matrix to indicate when each supervisory responsibility must be accomplished. Responsibilities usually are required on a per application or a monthly, quarterly or annual basis.

- Reorganize the list by the date responsibilities must be carried out. Begin with the most frequent activities.

- Identify who is responsible for the activity and enter the name in the matrix.

- Create a binder or file so that this information is easy to find.

- Create a compliance calendar based on the information. This annual calendar should indicate the date by which supervisory activities are required, files must be updated and reports must be provided. This calendar can be a useful tool for organizing the activities of the general agent or agency manager and staff.

The resulting matrix will provide a powerful road map for the general agent or agency manager to organize supervisory responsibilities. Appendix A provides an example of a responsibility matrix.

4. Identify the guidelines that must be followed in carrying out these responsibilities. Now that the general agent or agency manager has a concise list of responsibilities, he or she can use it to organize supervisory activities by doing the following:

- Make copies of company procedures and policies that provide directions for carrying out supervisory responsibilities.

- Make copies of all reports and annotate them to identify the key data that must be reviewed and the meaning of the data. For example, if data on persistency in an agency or office productivity report is used quarterly to identify potential market conduct issues, highlight the column of persistency data and identify the actions that might be taken depending on the level of each agent's persistency.

- Make copies of the forms and reports that must be completed and submitted to a company or maintained in the files. Obtain properly completed examples of all forms and reports to serve as references or templates.

The information collected and organized through this process serves as good documentation that the general agent or agency manager has formalized supervisory responsibilities. Should anyone question the general agent or agency manager's commitment to supervising compliance and market conduct, this process is evidence that responsibility for supervision has been taken seriously.

5. Identify where agency or office procedures do not correspond to company policies or procedures or state or NASD regulations.

While identifying responsibilities, the general agent or agency manager also should identify potential inconsistencies between actual agency or office practices and company requirements. For example, a company procedure may require that agent correspondence files be reviewed every month. In completing the matrix, the general agent or agency manager may realize that such reviews have not always been taking place every month or that a required correspondence log was not maintained. These potential inconsistencies should be identified and noted on a separate list for future action.

POTENTIAL SUPERVISORY CHALLENGE'S

Being Objective

Being objective when evaluating your own supervisory practices or office procedures can challenging. Such assessments are difficult, because they are part science and part art. Judgments of what is and is not appropriate sometimes are difficult. There may be a temptation to minimize the gap between the standards in this guide, state regulations or company policies and the agency or office's actual practices or a tendency to make excuses for gaps or to apply a lower standard. For example, a general agent may identify that a company procedure is not being followed as frequently as required, but rationalize that the agency or office really does not need the procedure because it is populated with highly experienced professionals. Or a general agent or agency manager may feel that supervising delegated activities is not needed because of the qualifications of the person to whom he or she has delegated the responsibility. Although such behavior is common and understandable, a self-assessment by someone who is unwilling to find areas for improvement likely will not provide positive benefits.

One way to address the need for objectivity is to rely on documentation, checklists and written standards. This guide provides many tools that support objectivity. The general agent or agency manager should contact the companies he or she has relationships with to get any guidelines or tools available to conduct the self-assessment. When preparing for the self-assessment, these should be reviewed to select the ones most applicable to the agency or office. For example, the general agent or agency manager may want to obtain a copy of the Insurance Marketplace Standards Association's handbook to review their standards.

Another way to ensure objectivity is to have parts of the assessment reviewed by another general agent, agency manager or qualified professional who can provide feedback on whether standards are being applied consistently and appropriately.

Taking Timely Action

Another challenge for the general agent or agency manager who does a self-assessment is that once a potential issue, inconsistency or development need is identified, action must be taken to resolve it. Failure to take action on a potential issue gives the appearance that it is an accepted practice. This can put the general agent or agency manager at risk of greater sanctions because the impropriety was known. Unless the general agent or agency manager is willing to take action based on findings, he or she should carefully consider the value in undertaking a self-assessment. In addition, some general agent or agency manager contracts require that the general agent and agency manager notify the company upon discovering potential improprieties. Failure to do so can lead to company sanctions and disciplinary actions.

Finding the Time

For some general agents and agency managers the most daunting barrier to conducting a self-assessment is finding the time and resources to conduct the assessment. General agents and agency managers who have limited administrative support may find that devoting time and energy to a self-assessment can hinder productivity. Though the simplest strategy is to stop all other activities to concentrate on the assessment, this is often is impractical. Following are tips for general agents or agency managers on how to develop a strategy for assessing their supervisory systems:

- If you have an administrative staff, get them involved. Delegate the basics of developing the matrix to them and have them present their results to you. This may help improve objectivity.

- Tie the assessment process into the normal agency or office annual planning process rather than letting it be an interruption to normal agency or office operations.

- If the general agent or agency manager has relationships with several companies, it may be easier to do the assessment one company at a time rather than for all companies at once.

- Collect all of the information that will be needed in advance. It often wastes time to have to stop the process to seek out information from a particular company.

- Find a college student who could help with the assessment as part of an internship.

Allowing Inconsistencies Because Company Standards Differ

When reviewing the completed responsibility matrix, some general agents or agency managers are struck by the differences between companies in their supervisory requirements. For example, one company may require the general agent or agency manager (or a designee) to review every application; another may not require that any be reviewed. If, in lieu of a consistent policy and procedure to review all applications, the general agent or agency manager only meets the minimum requirements of each company, the following can happen:

- Agents will notice that some companies have lower standards than others and they may gravitate to those companies. This will increase compliance risk.

- When the general agent or agency manager carries out the supervisory responsibilities for companies with higher standards, agents may challenge him or her by pointing out that other companies do not have such high standards. This can put the general agent or agency manager on the defensive.

- The general agent or agency manager will have different procedures for different companies. A proliferation of policies and procedures can complicate the task of efficiently supervising agent activity and compliance. For example, different compliance procedures for different companies may lead to confusion and errors.

Sometimes it is more efficient to have one set of procedures based on the company with the highest standards. The general agent or agency manager should consider this when developing enhancements to supervisory policies and procedures.

HOW TO CREATE A MONITORING AND SUPERVISORY SYSTEM

Simply having a responsibility matrix does not mean that a general agent or agency manager has a supervisory system. A compliance and market conduct supervisory system should have the following characteristics:

- documented and recorded;
- efficient;
- integrated into normal agency operations;
- carried out at the right times;
- conforms to all company requirements;
- conforms to all regulatory standards;
- focused on the right issues; and
- periodically evaluated and modified to improve effectiveness.

A review of these characteristics should help general agents and agency managers identify additional enhancements that can be made to their current supervisory processes and procedures.

Documented and Recorded

Documentation of a supervisory process is critical because it can demonstrate how the system was designed, how it operates and can provide evidence that it was used consistently. Maintaining timely records is tangible evidence that supervisory responsibilities were carried out. Documentation is critical to counter allegations that the general agent or agency manager failed to properly supervise the agents and administrative staff.

A documented process also allows greater ease in delegating tasks, following up on them and evaluating whether or not the compliance process is functioning properly.

Much of the documentation already has been collected through the process of developing the responsibility matrix. The documentation should answer these basic questions:

- Who is responsible for what?
- What supervisory activities must be carried out?
- Where are activities performed?
- Where are materials and records maintained?
- When do supervisory activities take place?

- Why are supervisory activities carried out?

- How are supervisory activities carried out?

Documentation should be organized. Some general agents and agency managers organize their supervisory activities according to major functions (see Appendix A for examples of categories); some according to company relationship; yet others based on when supervisory activities must be accomplished—daily activities in one file, weekly in another, and so on. Some use a binder with tabs to organize information; others use a filing cabinet with separate files.

A general agent or agency manager should tailor documentation to match his or her situation. Administrative staff who are assigned supervisory responsibility often can be helpful in creating and organizing proper documentation.

Efficient

Supervisory processes must be efficient to be implemented effectively. A cumbersome, inefficient system is a burden everyone will avoid.

In terms of supervisory processes, efficiency means that the activity is performed by the right person, paperwork is kept to a minimum, duplication and redundancy are avoided, information is handled once and the activity is documented once. In this way, time and energy are not spent on unimportant aspects of the task of supervision.

One of the most important things a general agent or agency manager can do is to streamline supervisory processes and procedures. Streamlining is perhaps the most valuable enhancement a general agent or agency manager can make to the supervisory system.

Before attempting to implement any changes, the general agent should involve agents and administrative staff in a brainstorming session to identify redundancy, duplication and waste. Needlessly complicated or complex supervisory procedures should be examined closely to determine ways to simplify them. The general agent or agency manager should contact the companies he or she has a relationship with, question them about their required processes and procedures and challenge them to help streamline the burdensome ones. Not all processes and procedures are required by regulations, and companies have flexibility in how their processes operate. Sometimes companies do not realize how cumbersome their processes and procedures are. Feedback from general agents and agency managers can lead to improvements.

The following are some ideas of ways to streamline supervisory processes. Not all will be applicable to every general agent or agency manager:

- Identify a single set of application review points that satisfies all companies rather than using different review points for each company.

- Identify redundant reports that must be filed with a company and determine how to consolidate them into one submission.

- Identify the primary reasons that the home office questions business and develop procedures that screen applications before submission so delays and follow-up are reduced.

- Schedule regular supervisor reviews based on the availability of monitoring information. Avoid conducting multiple reviews based on only one company's information.

- Identify one central point in the agency or office where copies of correspondence must be forwarded to be reviewed before being sent. Train several people to review correspondence so no delay occurs if one person is out of the office.

- Provide agents with a list of the key compliance issues that will trigger a delay in processing and show them how to avoid them. If agents or administrative staff believe an application or policy change will be delayed because of a compliance issue, have them provide an explanation in advance.

- Develop a compliance scorecard that allows the supervisor to have a one-page snapshot of critical compliance information that can be used to identify potential compliance issues.

- Provide agents with a list of the key things reviewed in an audit and encourage them to have their operation in order in advance of a planned audit.

- Have a single source for sales materials in the office so it can be updated and maintained easily.

- Set up a specific time each week to review sales materials that agents want approved by the home office. Communicate this time to the agents so they can provide materials before that date and avoid delays in having the material sent to the home office.

- Develop a compliance calendar for the agency or office and circulate it widely so that agents and administrative staff know the dates for compliance activities far in advance.

Delegating Responsibility for Compliance Supervision

One way to improve efficiency is to delegate some supervisory responsibilities to appropriate people in the agency. Though the general agent or agency manager typically has ultimate responsibility for compliance and market conduct, he or she can appropriately carry out that responsibility by closely supervising someone to whom he or she delegated the activity.

Being able to delegate some supervisory activities depends on the size of the agency or office and its administrative and management staff's level of experience. Managers should guard against delegating supervisory activities to someone who does not have the experience, knowledge or position in the agency or office to be effective. This action could be seen as undermining the importance of compliance efforts.

Delegating compliance activities frees up some of the general agent or agency manager's time. Routine or administrative supervisory responsibilities are good candidates for delegation because they require less skill to be carried out.

Sometimes it is a good idea to delegate responsibility to someone who does not receive an override, split commission or bonus on an agent's business, because it removes the potential conflict of interest inherent in the general agent or agency manager's position. Delegating responsibility can thereby lead to greater objectivity. It can be valuable to have someone carry out a supervisory activity and then have the general agent or agency manager review what was done.

A general agent or agency manager who is going to delegate responsibility for significant aspects of compliance and market conduct supervision and monitoring may do the following to help ensure that the delegated responsibilities are carried out properly:

- Develop a written description of the delegated activities, for example, "review applications daily for suitability and completion using appropriate company checklists and red flag indicators."

- Include in the description how the individual should carry out the delegated activities, for example, "maintain confidentiality of information, avoid any favoritism, immediately report to the general agent any potential compliance issues."

- Document the steps or process the individual must use to carry out those activities, including any procedures that must be created to document their actions and accomplishments.

- Identify and then provide the training needed to carry out the delegated activities effectively.

- Develop procedures to ensure that the individual who has been delegated activities receives all communication relevant to their responsibilities.

- Develop standards used to evaluate how well the individual carries out the delegated activities.

- Let agency or office staff know that the individual responsible for duties has the general agent or agency manager's full support in carrying them out.

- When the activities are first delegated, monitor them closely to ensure that they are being carried out effectively. Provide additional training if needed.

- Develop and document the process the general agent or agency manager will use to monitor and supervise how the individual carries out the delegated activities.

- Monitor and supervise (for example, review, evaluate and provide feedback) how well the delegated activities were carried out and document the supervision.

- Evaluate whether the delegated activities were carried out efficiently and modify the process to improve efficiency.

- Identify how the performance of the person delegated to carry out the activities that will impact compensation.

Depending on the activities that were delegated, it can be helpful to train another person to serve as a backup when the person who is primarily responsible is not available.

In addition, a general agent or agency manager should check with his or her broker-dealer regarding the propriety of delegating certain tasks. For example, the general agent or agency manager may not be allowed to delegate certain responsibilities to someone on the administrative staff unless that person is a registered representative of the broker-dealer. Some companies provide a list of activities that are appropriate to delegate and the type of person that could be given them. This list should be obtained and used.

Integrated Into Normal Agency Operations

Compliance and market conduct supervision and monitoring should be part of normal agency or office operation, not add-ons. Separating compliance supervision from normal supervisory activities creates the impression that it is an afterthought, or worse, an unnecessary burden on agents and administrative staff. This can create a barrier to effective supervision. For example, if normal productivity and performance reviews do not include compliance supervision, it may seem unimportant. Or if compliance activities are not carried out unless there is an imminent company audit, the wrong message may be sent. Some general agents and agency managers treat compliance supervision as the process of finding something "wrong" and may fail, therefore, to provide positive feedback when no problems exist. A general agent or agency manager should provide as much praise for a well-run agent practice as he or she does for consistent good sales performance.

However, compliance and market conduct supervision should be kept in perspective. The agent's primary function is to sell products and services to meet clients' needs. Compliance and market conduct supervision is a control function. If it is overemphasized or becomes a barrier to selling products and services, it is self-defeating.

Maintaining the right balance can sometimes be difficult. One way to determine whether the general agent or agency manager is maintaining the right balance is to ask agents and administrative staff. Their feedback and general good common sense can be used to achieve balance.

Carried Out At the Right Times

Compliance and market conduct supervision should be carried out when it can be most effective according to company, agency or office policy. For example, if persistency data is provided on a quarterly basis, reviewing it more frequently than this is not effective. If each application is to be screened for suitability before being submitted, it is inappropriate to submit the business and review it later. If possible errors exist, they should have been caught before the application was submitted. If an agent has committed a possible compliance error, action should be taken as soon as possible to correct it. Waiting to take action may turn a possible problem into an actual one that requires more serious remedial treatment.

As simple as it seems, it can be difficult to achieve proper timing. General agents and managers often are under severe time pressures. They may lack enough time to accomplish everything they must do.

Good organization is key to successful management, and compliance supervision is no exception. General agents and agency managers should construct a compliance calendar, detailed earlier in this guide, to help organize their time. It should outline when supervisory activities are required, files must be updated, reports must be provided, etc. The general agent or agency manager should supervise and monitor according to a written plan. Steps should be followed in the right order. Time should be set aside to review information before it must be acted on. Activities should be carried out at the right time—not too soon and not too late. Supervising only when an error has been discovered or when an examination or audit is about to be conducted is not effective.

Conforms to All Company Requirements and Regulatory Standards

The general agent or agency manager's supervisory procedures should meet or exceed the requirements of each company with which he or she has a relationship. It is important to determine periodically whether the agency or office's processes and procedures are meeting company standards. This is one of the purposes of company audits or examinations. Even if the agency or office is not subject to company audits, the general agent or agency manager should keep in mind the need to ensure that agency or office procedures are modified along with company policies.

Some general agents or agency managers conduct an evaluation six months before an annual audit to have enough time to make any necessary enhancements. Those who are not subject to company audits may perform this check annually when they conduct their own audit of agency or office procedures.

The compliance-savvy general agent or agency manager avoids the potential risks inherent in a particular company's low standards. Low standards can be easier to meet, but they do not reduce compliance risk.

General agents and agency managers also should be aware that not every company procedure and policy is determined by state or NASDR regulations. Company policies and procedures can be challenged because they are not always based on regulations. General agents and agency managers should not assume that every company requirement is inflexible. Companies can make exceptions and modify standards if doing so will not cause them to violate statutory or regulatory standards.

Focused on the Right Issues

An effective compliance supervisory system focuses on the right issues. An effective system must be tailored to the agents, their markets and the operation of the agency or office. Supervising the wrong issues or activities is a waste of precious time and energy. Using supervisory procedures that are not appropriate to the agency or office also wastes time and does not reduce compliance risk.

Three key criteria that will help you focus on the right issues are the:

- potential compliance risk of the activity;
- frequency of the activity; and
- level of experience of the agent involved.

The following examples will provide clarification:

- A high-risk activity, such as the replacement of life insurance policies owned by seniors, that occurs frequently in the agency or office and is carried out by relatively inexperienced agents needs attention. A supervisory procedure based on a careful review of each sale as well as trends in sales would be appropriate. The frequency of the activity and its potential risk make an annual review of a sampling of cases inadequate.

- If all agents are highly experienced, requiring them to attend classroom training on compliance may not be the best way to supervise training. It may be better to let them study the training on their own and sign a training log when they complete it.

- If the majority of agents sell less than five percent of policies to seniors, it may not make sense to review every agent's applications using a senior red flag indicator. If a market requires additional scrutiny because of high market conduct risk, only those agents who sell in that particular market should receive the added scrutiny.

- If no one in the agency or office has a web site, including a review of web traffic in a monthly supervisory report makes no sense.

- Reviewing persistency quarterly in a normally high persistency agency also is not the right issue. It would be more appropriate to review the agents whose persistency is below the agency average.

- It may be unwise to assume poor persistency simply because policies sold through work site marketing have a high lapse rate. Take care to avoid using the general or typical characteristics of a market as a rationalization for ignoring supervision.

A later section of this course provides specific advice on monitoring and supervising specific issues. This advice can help you focus on the right issues.

Periodically Evaluated and Modified to Improve Effectiveness

A supervisory system must be periodically evaluated to find where it does and does not work. Based on that evaluation, the system is modified to enhance and strengthen it. A good compliance supervisory system takes time to develop and perfect.

General agents and agency managers take the following steps to improve their compliance supervisory systems:

- step back and assess the system's effectiveness;
- identify areas for improvement;
- identify enhancements;
- test the enhancements' effectiveness;
- gain acceptance from those affected; and
- implement enhancements.

Sometimes it is difficult to identify the strengths and weaknesses of a system. One can be tempted to leave a system or process alone because it is working relatively well. It may not be working as well as it could, but there may not be a lot of energy to spare to refine it. This is especially true because general agents and agency managers are so pressed for time. However, compliance and market conduct supervision is so important that it deserves the investment of time and energy to maximize its effectiveness and efficiency.

Efficiency and ease of use usually can be improved. General agents and agency managers should listen closely to criticism about the amount of time and effort agents, administrative staff and managers are putting into supervision and monitoring compliance. From the perspective of agents and administrative staff, difficulty of use is the most frequently identified barrier to supervisory systems.

General agents and agency managers should ask their agents and administrative staff to critique the system and identify ways to improve it. It is especially important to ask for feedback from the people to whom responsibility for implementation has been delegated. This does not require a form or special process. It requires only that the general agent and agency manager ask for feedback and listen to it objectively.

Objectivity can be hard to accomplish. Sometimes managers discount employee comments by assuming they do not understand the importance of compliance and market conduct. General agents and agency managers also are sometimes defensive about their systems and procedures and avoid seeking criticism. General agents and agency managers must push themselves to ask for feedback, otherwise improvement may be impossible.

Testing potential enhancements before implementation is an important part of improving a current supervisory system. Sometimes what looks like a good idea on paper turns out to be terrible in practice. Any enhancements to a currently functioning supervisory system should be piloted before being implemented in the entire agency or office.

Finally, the general agent or agency manager who is savvy about compliance and market conduct knows that, even when an enhancement will lead to greater efficiency or ease of use, agent and staff support is still necessary. Selling the enhancement's value, therefore, can be important. Investing time in communicating the benefits of the enhancement will pay dividends when it is accepted without resistance.

KEY SPECIFIC MONITORING ISSUES

Now we will consider how to monitor and supervise specific market conduct and compliance issues. The issues we will discuss are:

- suitability;
- replacements;
- persistency;
- sales material use;
- proper disclosure;
- proper completion of applications and forms;
- money laundering; and
- licensing.

This list is not exhaustive. Depending on specific circumstances, a general agent or agency manager should identify any other important issues to supervise.

MONITORING SUITABILITY

Why

The basic suitability analysis focuses on whether the product recommended to a client meets the client's needs and objectives appropriately. Suitability should be monitored because it increasingly is seen as a market conduct issue for regulators, plaintiffs' counsels and companies. Questions about suitability often are raised long after the sale, when information may no longer be available or memories about the specific sale may have faded. It is best to address suitability issues when the initial recommendation or sale is made.

Companies are beginning to include language about suitability in their contracts and selling agreements, while others believe the language in their current contracts requires the general agent or agency manager to take responsibility for monitoring suitability.

The NASDR requires a review of the suitability of a variable product's investment aspects. NASDR Conduct Rule 2310 (Suitability) requires that, when a recommendation is made to a customer regarding the purchase, sale or exchange of any security (which includes variable insurance products), the registered representative must have reasonable grounds for believing that the recommendation is suitable for the customer, based on the facts disclosed by the customer. The broker-dealer's registered principal is responsible to conduct this analysis and must endorse the recommendation. In addition, the NASDR also has recommended that the broker-dealer review the more general aspects of suitability for sales (e.g., whether the product appropriately meets the client's needs). NASDR Notice to Members 99-35 and

> **ILL. 5.1 ■ *It's All About the Agent***
>
> The general agent and agency manager should keep in mind that the primary responsibility for determining suitability lies with the agent. The agent has the most data on and insight into the client's needs. The purpose of monitoring suitability is to identify potential instances where the basis for the recommendation or sale is unclear or potentially improper. The general agent or agency manager should be careful not to assume responsibility for determining the suitability of a recommendation or sale unless he or she was privy to all that occurred during all sales interviews.

00-44 address variable annuity and variable life sales. In addition, Notice to Members 96-86 reminds members that the sale of variable contracts are subject to NASDR suitability requirements.

State regulators are looking closely at developing suitability guidelines and regulations. The NAIC has a committee studying the subject. At the writing of this book, however, final model regulations from the NAIC were not completed. Some states have developed suitability regulations, and those regulations should be followed by the agent in all applicable sales.

When

Suitability data usually should be reviewed on a case-by-case basis to fully understand their meaning and provide the earliest warning of potential compliance concerns. This is required for variable sales.

If the general agent or agency manager evaluates the suitability of applications before they are submitted to a company, he or she should conduct an evaluation on a timely basis to avoid delays in submitting the case or application. This can put pressure on a general agent or agency manager to do the evaluations quickly and on a regular (sometimes daily) basis. However, the general agent or agency manager has the best chance of avoiding potential suitability issues by evaluating applications before they are submitted. If questions arise, he or she can request additional information to ensure that the sale is suitable. Potential errors can be corrected much more easily before the application is submitted than afterwards.

However, for some agents, a periodic, random assessment of the broader concept of suitability (i.e., the aspects of suitability other than the suitability of the investment component which is required by the NASDR for every sale) may be appropriate.* For example, a review of 20 percent of the cases written every quarter may be sufficient for experienced agents who have demonstrated in the past that they carefully consider suitability and maintain comprehensive case documentation. A periodic

---

* For additional information on the concept of suitability, see Dennis M. Groner, *Practical Compliance for Insurance Professionals* (LIMRA International: Hartford, CT, 2001).

review of suitability may allow the general agent or agency manager to examine the entire client file more carefully as part of an evaluation.

For agents who place business with a broker-dealer who reviews variable product suitability in the home office, a more extensive review of suitability may be necessary annually or semi-annually only.

For agents whose cases are reviewed for suitability periodically, additional emphasis on suitability should be made whenever a new product is introduced, because a major product change can lead to potential suitability issues. This additional emphasis should be kept in place until the agents have demonstrated that they have mastered the product.

How

The sources of information that are used to assess suitability come from the application and case documentation. A good source of information for assessing suitability is the need analysis data collected by the agent. This can be especially useful if a computer-based data collection and analysis program is used. Another good source of data is a written report, discovery agreement or recommendation. However, unless the general agent or agency manager requires that this data be provided with the application (e.g., the entire client file), he or she may have only the application data on which to rely. For variable product applications, this may include the new client form, which typically is useful only for assessing the suitability of the investment choices. Company applications and forms may not provide enough data to assess the overall suitability of the recommendation.

An alternative way to obtain data to evaluate suitability is to ask the agent to provide a summary of key information on each case. The suitability review checklist presented in Ill. 5.2 is an example of a summary form that can be used. If the agent is not required to provide the checklist, the general agent or agency manager still can use the questions listed on it as a basis for evaluation of suitability. In addition to the information evaluated on the checklist, the general agent or agency manager should consider any company or NASD requirements for the application.

Even with this checklist, case or application analysis requires experience and knowledge. It may be difficult to delegate this analysis because of the background required to do it properly.

For variable products, the registered principal is required to endorse the suitability of the sale, especially its investment aspects, before its submission. The manager may or may not be the registered representative's registered principal. The suitability review checklist contains questions aimed at supporting the evaluation of the suitability of registered product sales, but the manager who is a registered principal should contact his or her broker-dealer to determine the required process.

If the general agent or agency manager requires the agent to provide a summary with each application, he or she should also require the agent to sign the checklist, thereby attesting to its accuracy. Care should be taken not to allow someone who is not familiar with the case to provide the information, e.g., the agent's administrative staff.

ILL 5.2 ■ *Suitability Review Checklist*

Answer Yes, No or N/A (Not Applicable) to each question based on your knowledge of the circumstances of the sale. If your answer to any question is in a shaded box, you should review your recommendation. An answer in a shaded box does not mean that the recommendation is unsuitable, it only means that you should carefully analyze the suitability of your recommendation. You may want to provide additional documentation containing information supporting your recommendation along with the application.

This checklist is intended solely to serve as a tool to help producers assess and review suitability before submission of an application.

Review Questions	Yes	No	N/A
1. Have you collected adequate information about the client to determine his or her objectives, needs, financial circumstances and risk tolerance?			
2. Have you adequately documented and analyzed the information collected to reach a well-reasoned, logical recommendation?			
3. Is some product other than life insurance or an annuity more suitable given the client's objectives, needs, financial circumstances and risk tolerance?			
4. Does the recommendation take into account the other financial products currently owned by the client?			
5. Can the client understand the features, options and operation of the product being recommended?			
6. If the client likely will be rated due to health, has the client been advised of that possibility?			
7. Is the premium greater than 15 percent of the client's liquid net worth?			
8. Is the annual premium greater than 10 percent of the client's annual income or household income?			
9. If the client is over age 60, does he or she have a need for the life insurance protection offered by the product?			
10. If the client is over age 60, is he or she likely to have a need for the funds accumulating or invested in the product during the period when withdrawal and surrender charges apply?			
11. Have the tax implications of the recommended product been evaluated in terms of the client's current and future situation?			
12. If the product has flexible payment options, is the initial minimum or guideline premium great enough to maintain the product in force to age 99?			
If a variable product is being recommended, the following questions should be reviewed:			
13. Are the client's risk tolerance and investment objectives consistent with one another?			
14. Is the client's selection of investment options consistent with his or her risk tolerance and investment objectives?			
15. Does the client understand the risks associated with the investment options he or she is considering?			
16. Is the drop-in amount greater than 20 percent of the client's liquid net worth?			

In addition to the case or application review, data can be analyzed to identify potential suitability issues. Following are some example questions that could be asked based on the data some companies make available to general agent or agency managers. The general agent or agency manager should use his or her experience and knowledge of his or her agents, products, etc., to tailor the analysis.

Some companies use a post-sale client survey (e.g., the LIMRA Customer Assurance Program or one of their own design) to determine whether a needs analysis was conducted during the sale or if the client feels his or her needs were met by the product. Data from these surveys can be useful in identifying potentially unsuitable sales. If a company provides this data, they should be reviewed on a periodic basis to identify trends.

The following questions will be helpful in compiling data concerning suitability issues:

- **Which agents have a significant number of pending applications?** Large numbers of pending applications (i.e., applications where additional data, forms, etc., are required) may reflect an unwillingness to contact clients, which may suggest the initial sale may not have been based on a proper needs analysis.

- **How long have case or application requirements been outstanding?** The longer the average time period, the more likely the producer may be unwilling to meet with the client. Sometimes this may be a reflection on the suitability of the recommendation.

- **Which agents have a significant number of clients who declined the policy after it was issued?** A high percentage of declined policies may reflect unsuitable or high pressure sales. Some companies will survey clients who have declined issued policies to determine the reason.

- **What is the agent's lapse rate?** Lapses may provide an indicator of sales that were not suitable or needs based. For example, some first-year lapses result from failing to do a need analysis, which may lead to selling more coverage than the client can afford. Using a high-pressure sales process also may lead to a high first-year lapse rate. See the section on persistency for additional information on how persistency data can indicate potential compliance issues.

- **Are a significant percentage of the agent's clients late in paying their premiums?** Some companies provide late payment reports. Late payments by clients can suggest potentially unsuitable sales.

- **Are lapses concentrated among an entire family?** This may indicate a strong negative reaction to the producer. There may be a significant problem below the surface, such as unsuitable sales or high-pressure sales tactics.

- **Are policies delivered on time?** Companies that require delivery receipts sometimes provide data on delays in receiving signed delivery receipts. If an agent frequently has to be reminded to submit delivery receipts it may indicate policy sales based on potentially unsuitable recommendations.

- **Does the agent conduct regular reviews of client needs?** Suitability typically does not end with the sale. Part of suitability is the regular review of client needs. Sometimes it is difficult to get this data. When doing case review, the general agent or agency manager can ask the agent to share his or her process for following up on clients' needs.

In addition to these kinds of data, client questions directed to the agent's administrative staff sometimes indicate potential suitability issues. Another sign of an unsuitable sale is when clients repeatedly question the agent about the product and how it meets their needs. The easiest way to get this data is to ask the administrative staff to let the general agent or agency manager know if an agent has been getting a lot of telephone calls from clients asking the agent to explain the product they purchased.

Based on suitability data, the general agent or agency manager may identify a potential compliance or market conduct issue but be uncertain of its validity. To investigate further, it may be valuable to contact clients to find out why lapses occurred, payments were late, etc. This information can help further clarify a question about a potential compliance issue.

To help put their own agency or office data in perspective (e.g., average agency persistency), general agents and agency managers should obtain the company averages for other agencies or offices, Care must be taken in using this information. Sometimes it is unclear whether the company average can be applied to the general agent and agency manager's agency or office. Size, market, geographical location, etc., are important factors that can influence the meaning of company averages. If the general agent or agency manager has a number of relationships with companies, it is important to consider which company's averages to use.

A general agent or agency manager should maintain an ongoing record of how he or she evaluated the suitability of cases or applications so that it can be used to spot trends. For example, an agent may sell only 10 policies each year to elderly clients. However, every one of those sales may suggest potential suitability issues. The general agent or agency manager should be able to document and track suitability analyses, so that he or she can spot this type of trend. He or she may want to maintain a database on the cases analyzed to better monitor trends. If the general agent or agency manager uses a periodic case review process, identifying trends is somewhat easier, because he or she may be better able to see a pattern that took place in the past.

Suitability monitoring data, summaries, etc., should be maintained in the general agent or agency manager's compliance files and updated regularly.

MONITORING REPLACEMENTS

Why

Monitoring replacements also is an important element of an overall monitoring and supervision system. Replacement abuses can involve both life insurance and annuities.

Replacement refers to any transaction in which a new policy or contract is to be purchased, and it is known or should be known to the proposing producer, or to the proposing insurer if there is no producer, that by reason of the transaction, an existing policy or contract has been or is to be:

- lapsed, forfeited, surrendered or partially surrendered, assigned to the replacing insurer or otherwise terminated;

- converted to reduced paid-up insurance, continued as extended term insurance, or otherwise reduced in value by the use of nonforfeiture benefits or other policy values;

- amended so as to effect either a reduction in benefits or in the term for which coverage would otherwise remain in force or for which benefits would be paid;

- reissued with any reduction in cash value; or

- used in a financed purchase.*

Replacement activity includes both internal replacements—when the policies or contracts affected are all within the same underwriting company—and external replacements—when non-affiliated companies underwrite the affected policies or contracts.

The NASDR covers replacements under NASDR Conduct Rule 2310 (the suitability rule). For additional information see Notice to Members 01-23. In addition, in Notice to Members 99-35, the NASDR advised broker-dealers to conduct careful reviews of variable annuity 1035 exchanges. The NASDR's Notice to Members 00-44 advised broker-dealers to include in their heightened review of variable life insurance sales whether registered representatives had carefully considered that a replacement was in the best interest of the client before making a recommendation. Both of these notices directed broker-dealers to exercise closer supervision and monitoring of replacement activity.

The NASDR's Investor Alert was concerned with variable annuity exchanges.** The alert contained a discussion of the costs and benefits of making a replacement or exchange and a warning that an exchange might not be in the client's best interest.

Replacements have been and continue to be a serious market conduct issue. Regulators and companies have been vigilant in identifying replacement abuses. Companies routinely hold general agents and agency managers responsible for improper replacements based on the typical clause in their contracts and selling agreements related to complying with laws and regulations. Companies are required (by state laws and regulations and IMSA, which many belong to) to have policies and

---

* Adapted from the NAIC Model Replacement Regulation, 1998, Section 2.J. Specific state regulations may vary. For additional information on replacements, see Dennis M. Groner, *Practical Compliance for Insurance Professionals* (LIMRA International: Hartford, CT, 2001).

** "Should You Exchange Your Variable Annuity," February 2001, available on the NASD official web site, http://www.nasdr.com/alert 0201/htm.

procedures in place to monitor and track replacements. These policies also are used as a basis for assigning responsibility for monitoring replacements to the general agent and agency manager.

When

To effectively monitor replacements, the manager should assess the appropriateness of all replacement activity regardless of the type of policy, experience of the producer, market, etc., before the application for a replacement is submitted or when changes to current policies are requested.

Replacement data should be reviewed on a case-by-case basis to fully understand their meaning and to provide an early warning of potential compliance concerns. Clients also can independently initiate activities that can be related to replacements, e.g., requesting a loan on policy values.

How

General agents and agency managers typically must begin their supervision by reviewing the following for all replacements:

- Were the required state and company forms included with the application?

- Were the required forms completed properly?

- Does the producer have sufficient information to demonstrate the suitability of the replacement?

Required State and Company Forms

Some states require that comparison forms be completed for all replacements. Some companies require that their own forms be completed for every replacement. In some cases, this may involve two or more separate forms.

A significant part of a general agent or agency manager's review is to ensure that any required state or company forms are provided with the application and have been completed correctly. This responsibility can be delegated to administrative staff with the proper controls and supervision. However, general agents and agency managers should make certain that whomever they delegate responsibility to has the knowledge and experience to properly review required forms.

Whoever does this review must know how to complete these forms properly. Information on how to complete state- and company-required forms should be obtained from the companies the agent has a relationship with or developed by the general agent or agency manager. For example, some companies provide a list of the required company and state forms for each major type of replacement, e.g., permanent life to permanent life replacements, permanent life to term life replacements, etc. Others provide charts that show state and company requirements.

A Checklist for Reviewing Whether Replacement Documentation Is Complete

A general agent or agency manager is wise to develop reference materials to help ensure that he or she knows state and company requirements. For example, some general agents and agency managers create a checklist of required items:

1. Is a current version of State Form (X) attached to application?

2. Is a current version of Company Form (Y) attached to application?

3. Is client information on the state form identical to the information on the company form and application?

4. Is agent's signature present and appropriately dated?

5. Are clients' signatures present and appropriately dated?

6. Do all signatures match the signatures on the application?

7. Are sales materials used in the sale attached, including any illustrations?

8. Are numerical entries on state and company forms based on either a current illustration, the original policy or a company authorized printout?

9. Is a copy of the policy to be replaced attached.?

It also can be useful to create templates or models of completed forms to serve as reference materials and to provide agents with guidance on completing the forms and administrative staff with guidance on conducting the review.

Though some companies review this information whenever an application involving a replacement is submitted, it is wise not to rely completely on a home office or company review to identify potential incomplete, inconsistent or missing information. Reliance on company reviews may lead to delays in approving the application because of difficulty communicating with the agent.

The Replacement Log

The review of the required forms should be documented. This can involve the administrative staff completing a company-required form, initialing and dating a cover sheet to the application, etc. In addition, some companies require that a replacement log be maintained, i.e., a list of all reviewed and submitted replacements. Such a log is a valuable tool for identifying trends in replacement activity and typically includes the:

- agent's name;

- client's name;

- date of review;

- company whose policy or contract is being considered for replacement;
- type of policy considered for replacement;
- company whose policy is being recommended;
- type of policy being recommended;
- result of the review;
- reasons for delaying application submission;
- name of reviewer;
- date application is submitted;
- company actions or questions; and
- policy issue date.

This log should be reviewed periodically to identify agents who are not providing complete or accurate documentation and should provide appropriate documentation that monitoring of replacements was carried out. The agency or office should maintain such a log even if companies with which the general agent or agency manager has a relationship do not require it.

Demonstrating the Suitability of a Replacement

The sources of information used to assess suitability come from application and case documentation. In addition to a thorough needs analysis, a comparative analysis of maintaining the original policy versus replacing it also may need to be conducted. This need not be a numerical analysis, though that may sometimes be necessary to demonstrate suitability.

Some state- or company-required forms require these analyses, which means that a careful review of them can serve as the basis for an assessment of the replacement's suitability.

A Replacement Screening Tool

To help in the process of reviewing the suitability of replacements, we provide a checklist in Ill. 5.3 that can be used to screen applications. It can help a general agent or agency manager evaluate or screen replacements to determine whether the information provided is sufficient to conclude that the replacement is in the client's best interest. Some companies provide checklists and guidelines for evaluating replacements. The general agent or agency manager should determine whether he or she is required to use specific guidelines of the company whose product is being sold or, in some cases, the company whose product is being used to fund a replacement.

ILL 5.3 ■ *Replacement Screen*

Consequences to be Considered	Yes	No
1. Modifications to the current policy will enable the client to pay the current premium, but it is unclear how future premiums will be paid.		
2. The additional coverage provided by the new policy does not appear to meet the financial needs or objectives of the client.		
3. The purchase of additional coverage through a contract provision does not appear to meet the financial needs or objectives of the client.		
4. A loss of cash value will occur due to initial first year expenses on the new policy or contract.		
5. The cost of insurance for the new policy or contract is higher than the original one.		
6. A new surrender or withdrawal charge period will begin with the new policy or contract.		
7. The new policy or contract has higher surrender or withdrawal charges than the original one.		
8. New evidence of insurability will be required.		
9. Premiums may be required for a longer period of time with the new policy or contract.		
10. A new contestability/suicide period will begin with the new policy or contract.		
11. The client can anticipate higher costs for insurance due to increased age, changes in health, etc.		
12. Guaranteed dividend or crediting rates are lower on the new policy or contract.		
13. The client will lose favorable contract provisions, options, benefits or guarantees.		
14. The new policy or contract has a higher interest loan rate than the original one.		
15. Administration or management fees on the new policy or contract are higher than on the original one.		
16. The client will experience unfavorable tax consequences on any gain from the existing policy or contract.		
17. The new policy or contract will require payment of new set-up or initiation fees.		
18. The new policy or contract will raise or create ownership questions or problems that did not exist with the original one.		
19. The new policy or contract will raise or create beneficiary questions or problems that did not exist with the original one.		
20. The use of funds from the original policy or contract to pay the premium on the new policy or to fund the original policy may create a potential lapse in the original policy.		

(This checklist is based on the form required by the NAIC model replacement regulation.)

For companies and states that do not require replacement forms, the general agent or agency manager can use the Replacement Screen checklist as a way to obtain information about the replacement and to document that monitoring took place.

The replacement screen checklist details the potential consequences of a replacement that can help identify whether it is suitable or in the client's interest. Every affirmative answer raises potential questions about the appropriateness of the replacement. However, judgment should be exercised to determine whether extenuating circumstances must be taken into consideration before considering the recommendation inappropriate. For every affirmative answer, the general agent or agency manager should have additional information from the agent that provides a logical and compelling reason why the replacement is suitable.

Some general agents and agency managers may request that the agent provide his or her answers to any affirmative answers on the checklist in writing; others will accept a verbal explanation. A written response ensures documentation of proper supervision. In some cases, this information is shared with the company whose product is being sold as a replacement. This can be accomplished by including the information on a required company form or by attaching a letter to the application containing the information. If this information is not shared with the company, it should be kept in the files of the agent and general agent or agency manager in case questions arise about the propriety of the replacement. An accurately completed and dated form should be adequate to demonstrate appropriate supervision of replacement suitability.

Even with this checklist, case or application analysis requires experience and knowledge. It may be difficult to delegate this analysis because of the background required to do it properly.

Tracking Trends in Replacement Activity

Replacement activity typically should be reviewed on a producer level to fully understand its meaning. This can be difficult unless the general agent or agency manager has well-organized data. Some companies provide reports that help organize this important data for internal and external replacements. For example, a common report provides information on internal and external replacement activity on a rolling quarter basis, which can show a four or six quarter trend of replacement activity. Another common report lists all client loan, withdrawal, surrender, etc., activity by agent, which can be useful in identifying potential hidden replacements.

General agents and agency managers should find out what reports are available from the companies with which their agents have a relationship. General agents and agency managers whose agents sell products from several companies are faced with the task of coordinating those reports to obtain a complete picture of an agent's overall replacement activity and to identify potential hidden replacements. If a company does not provide regular reports on replacements by agent, the general agent or agency manager may want to ask them to generate an ad hoc report quarterly or semi-annually to aid tracking trends in agent replacement activity.

General agents and agency managers should review replacement activity on a regular basis. The timing and frequency of this review sometimes will be determined by the time frames of the reports used. For example, if a general agent or agency manager receives quarterly reports on replacement activity, he or she should review replacement activity on a quarterly basis.

The following are examples of questions that could be asked using the data that companies typically make available to managers. The general agent or agency manager should use his or her experience and knowledge of the agents, products, etc., to tailor the analysis:

- Which agents have the largest percentage of replacements? Are they primarily internal or external replacements?

- Is the agent's percentage of internal and external replacements significantly higher than the company, agency or office average?

- Have any agents had recent, large increases in replacement activity either on a percentage or absolute basis?

- Was a new product recently introduced, and have a large number of contracts been replaced with the new product?

- Is there a trend or pattern in any of the following:

    - product being replaced;

    - number of years the replaced policy has been in force;

    - new product being sold;

    - age or location of the clients who are replacing policies;'

    - time of year; or

    - agent who originally wrote the policy.

- Is there a trend in the number of lapses from a group of agents? Do they all work in one location?

- Are the proceeds of surrendered policies being moved into mutual funds for a period of time and then used to purchase new policies?

- If replacements involve the use of policy values, how are they being accessed, (e.g., loans, partial surrenders, withdrawals, increases in face amount without an increase in premium, etc.)?

- Has loan activity increased among an agent's clients? Are loan amounts for whole numbers or for odd amounts? Is there a pattern of loans over a regular time period, (e.g., monthly, quarterly, semi-annually)?

- Are lapses among clients who have had policies in force for several years?

- Are clients who lapsed policies in one company the agent represents purchasing policies in another after a lag of several months?

- Are clients with several small face amount policies lapsing them all within a short period of time?

- If a company uses a new client survey, such as LIMRA's Customer Assurance Program (CAP) or one of their own design, do some agents have very low return rates? Low return rates may indicate that the agent is suggesting to clients not to submit the questionnaire, because it asks about replacements.

Based on replacement activity, a general agent or agency manager may identify a potential compliance or market conduct issue but be unsure of its validity. Sometimes it is valuable to contact clients to determine the circumstances surrounding a lapse, loan or replacement. If a general agent, agency manager or administrative staff person contacts clients, he or she must exercise great care to ask questions that do not generate any negative conclusions regarding the agent, agency, office or company in the mind of the client.

A general agent or agency manager should maintain an ongoing record of how he or she evaluated replacement activity so that it can be used to spot trends over a time period greater than the reports used. He or she should be able to document and track replacement activity analyses and to spot trends and patterns.

Some general agents and agency managers initial all replacement reports to demonstrate that they were reviewed. Others take notes on the reports to document their actions. Still others file a brief note of the result of their reviews and the actions taken on them.

Replacement monitoring information should be maintained in the general agent or agency manager's compliance files and updated regularly.

Identifying Undisclosed (Hidden) Replacements

An undisclosed or hidden replacement is when an agent knows that a replacement is taking place, but does not identify that fact, e.g., he or she fails to identify a replacement on the application or on a state or company required form. By doing so, an agent is in violation of state regulations and most companies' policies. One of the goals of replacement monitoring is to identify hidden or undisclosed replacements.

In some cases, the agent does not know that a client plans to lapse, surrender or borrow on a policy. Therefore, to protect themselves from being accused of hiding a replacement, agents should question clients to determine whether they plan to do so. It is wise to document both the questions and the client's answers.

To identify hidden or undisclosed internal replacements, some companies search their policy records for a period of time, often 13 months before and after the replacement activity, for lapses, surrenders, loans, withdrawals and other activity. Some companies, however, use longer timeframes of 25 or more months; if a state requires a longer time for the search, it should be used.

A company may be contacted by another company that believes an agent is replacing their policies without properly notifying them. One of the purposes of state replacement regulations is to ensure that the replaced company or organization receives proper notification. This is another way that the some companies identify hidden replacements.

Some companies survey policyholders (e.g., telephone surveys, printed surveys and questionnaires, such as LIMRA's CAP) following purchases and transactions, such as loan requests, lapses, etc., to determine whether there has been a replacement. One of the objectives of these programs is to identify hidden replacements.

Failure to disclose a replacement is a serious violation of state regulations and company policy that may lead to sanctions, including termination. Some companies alert general agents and agency managers to potential hidden replacement situations. When this occurs, the general agent or agency manager should follow the company's procedures for investigating a potential hidden replacement.

General agents and agency managers also should be sensitive to hidden replacements and review agent activity to identify them. If a general agent or agency manager suspects that a hidden replacement has taken place, he or she should investigate the circumstances. Once a hidden replacement is confirmed, he or she should contact the company whose product was sold or funded as a replacement and alert them. At that point, company policy should dictate what steps are taken.

MONITORING PERSISTENCY

Why

Keeping policies on the books should be the goal of every general agent and agency manager. Poor persistency costs agents, companies and management money.

However, poor persistency also costs agents the bond of trust with their clients. The decision to purchase insurance is based on trust. When clients lapse their policies or contracts, it may indicate that they felt their trust was misplaced. At the same time, policies lapse for many reasons that are not related to market conduct, e.g., job loss, divorce, changes in needs, etc. Persistency data can help a manager spot several key market conduct problems. Persistency data, like all indicators or measures, must be analyzed carefully to determine its meaning.

There is a demonstrated relationship between persistency and complaints. Research typically finds that the poorer the persistency of an agency or office, the higher the number of client complaints it receives. Client complaints sometimes indicate the presence of serious market conduct or compliance issues.

When

Persistency data should be reviewed on an agent-by-agent and overall agency or office basis to fully understand its meaning. If the agent has relationships with several companies, the timing of the persistency data review often will depend on when those companies provide data so that the agent's persistency can be assessed accurately. Though some companies provide persistency data monthly or quarterly, they more typically provide it annually or semi-annually. This suggests that reviews of persistency should be conducted annually or semi-annually, when the majority of reports are available.

How

For agent analyses, the data from as many companies as possible should be combined to draw as complete a picture as possible of an agent's overall pattern of persistency. Sometimes this presents a challenge to a general agent or agency manager who has relationships with many companies. Companies may define persistency differently, making direct comparisons of their data difficult, e.g., first-year lapse rate (less that 12 months), 13-month lapse rate, 24-month lapse rate, 4-year persistency, etc. In addition, persistency data should be compared to agency and company averages or standards. Different definitions of persistency can make these comparisons difficult.

For agency or office analyses, the overall agency or office data should be evaluated. Sometimes the general agent or agency manager must request this data, because some companies provide only agent reports. Again, different definitions of persistency can make it difficult to interpret the results.

The general agent or agency manager should use experience and knowledge of his or her agents, products, etc., to tailor the analysis. Many questions can be asked when analyzing persistency data.

On an Agent Basis

Which agents have a large number of lapses during the first or second year of a contract's life? Be sure to contrast the absolute number with the percentage of cases written during the same time period. A small increase can translate into a large percentage and not be as meaningful. Lapses during the first two years of a contract may indicate the following important compliance issues:

- Sudden increases in lapse rates or dramatically lower persistency may signal hidden replacements. The other sales activity of the agent should be examined to determine whether the same clients are subsequently purchasing new policies.

- Higher than average lapses of life insurance policies with considerable cash value may suggest hidden replacements. The other sales activity of the agent should be examined to determine whether the same clients are subsequently purchasing new policies.

- Higher than average lapses of life insurance policies with considerable cash value also may reflect a lack of follow-through or ongoing customer service. Low interest rates or dividend rates may make these policies ripe for external replacements.

- Higher than average first-year lapses may indicate suitability problems with the sale. For example, the agent may be selling polices that do not fulfill a client's needs or the agent's sales associates or staff may be selling policies without fully explaining them or providing proper follow-up. When it becomes clear to clients that their policy or contract does not meet their needs, they lapse the policy.

- High numbers of lapses within the first policy year also may indicate a high-pressure sales approach, which may be forcing clients to buy, only to lapse after a short period of time.

- Concentrations of lapses among an entire family may indicate a strong negative reaction to the agent. This could indicate a significant problem below the surface that can become a complaint.

- First-year lapses involving the same product may signal that the features, benefits and costs of new products are not being explained properly. The agent may not be knowledgeable enough about a new product, which leads to client expectations not being met, which may be causing the lapses.

- Poor persistency for an agent who sells large numbers of policies or contracts may indicate inadequate customer service or failure to conduct an effective delivery interview.

- Poor persistency for agents who do work-site marketing may indicate inadequate customer service or a failure to provide disclosure adequately at the time of sale.

On an Agency or Office Basis

What is the trend in lapses for the agency or office? How does the agency or office's persistency compare to other agencies or offices selling in the same markets? This data often can be obtained from the companies with which the agents have a relationship by examining the following issues:

- What are the common features of the clients or markets in which lapses are taking place? Are there similarities among the type of policy lapses or the type of client? For example, do the lapses include orphan or unassigned clients? Are the lapses from clients in a specific geographic area? Are the lapsed policies similar? Are there any consistent patterns or trends?

- Agencies or offices with high lapse rates may be using sales systems that are leading to potentially unsuitable sales, or agents may be trained improperly regarding suitability or product features.

- How much does the current data (e.g., lapse rate) differ from historical data (e.g., the prior year's results, company or agency averages, etc.)? Is the trend one of consistently deteriorating persistency? Is the change consistent across all agents, concentrated among a small group of agents or just one? Concentrations of lapses may signal that a group of agents are using improper sales methods or similar sales systems.

- How do the markets and sales of high-lapse agents differ from those of low-lapse agents? This comparison may take some work to develop, but it could demonstrate the underlying cause of deterioration in agency or office persistency.

- Increases in lapses of orphan policies may indicate that a former agent is replacing business without properly notifying the replaced company of the replacement.

Based on persistency data, the general agent or agency manager may identify a potential compliance or market conduct issue but be unsure of its validity. It is sometimes valuable to contact clients who have lapsed their policies or contracts over the past year to determine why the lapse occurred. This information can help clarify the situation further.

If the general agent, agency manager or administrative staff person contacts clients, he or she should exercise great care not to ask questions that generate any negative conclusions in the mind of the client about the agent, agency, office or company.

A general agent or agency manager should maintain an ongoing record of how he or she evaluated persistency data to demonstrate that it was reviewed. Some general agents and agency managers initial all persistency reports, while others take notes on the reports to document their actions. Still others file a brief note about the result of their review and the action taken.

Persistency monitoring information should be maintained in the general agent or agency manager's compliance files and updated regularly.

MONITORING SALES MATERIAL USE

Why

Sales materials are broadly defined as any material used to:

- present information to clients about products or services (e.g., web sites, signage, business cards);

- secure an appointment with clients, (e.g., agent brochures, direct mail letters, e-mail);

- conduct a sales presentation (e.g., sales presentations, data collection tools, seminar presentations);

- inform or educate clients (e.g., product brochures, descriptions of products, prospectuses); or

- document the sales process or recommendations if shared with the client (e.g., confirmation letters, reports).

All sales material used by agents should be approved in advance by the company whose product is being presented for sale. For registered products, the broker-dealer must approve the materials and then file them with the NASDR. The approval of sales materials is required by the NASDR and many states. Any sales materials used should be the most up-to-date version available. Failure to do so can give the impression that the agent is attempting to misrepresent the product's features, benefits or costs. It is considered a serious compliance and market conduct impropriety to use unapproved or outdated sales materials.*

When

Sales material use should be reviewed on an agent-by-agent basis as part of the general agent or agency manager's ongoing auditing program. Audits typically are performed on a semi-annual, annual or biennial basis. Reviews should be conducted whenever new sales materials are made available to agents or when periodic audits are conducted. Periodic reviews of sales materials managed by the agency or office should be conducted to remove outdated materials. Agency and office reviews should be conducted based on the frequency of updated company sales material listings and of the expiration dates of agent-, agency- or office-developed sales materials.

How

General agents and agency managers primarily monitor agent use of sales material through periodical audits or examinations of client files and the agent's office and supplies. This includes reviewing any computer-based sales materials and programs, e.g., computer based presentations.

Regardless of whether the sales material is found in a client file or on a shelf in the agency or office, there should be:

- company code that indicates approval printed on the copy; or
- a letter or notice in the files that the sales material is approved.

Audits of an agent's files and office should follow a checklist used to organize, guide and document the audit, a section of which should include sales material use. In addition to reviewing a sample of client files and the agent's office, the general agent or agency manager should interview the agent and his or her administrative staff regarding sales material use. Specific information on agent reviews or audits is discussed in a later section of this guide.

The following are some of the sales material use issues to consider:

- Agents should not use any materials with clients that have *For Internal Use Only, For Agent Use Only* or similar notice on them.

- Agents should not have personally reproduced copies of official company sales materials unless those copies are created through an approved process. It is typically improper to copy a company brochure unless controls are in place to ensure that the copy is identical to the original. Most companies do

---

* For additional information on sales material requirements and review procedures, see Dennis M. Groner, *Practical Compliance for Insurance Professionals* (LIMRA International: Hartford, CT, 2001).

not allow sales materials to be copied unless they are provided through a computer network.

- The general agent or agency manager should examine whether the sales materials in the file correspond to the products presented or sold. It is questionable to use one company's sales materials in the sale of another company's products. Even if the sales materials are generic, only the sales material related to the specific products recommended and sold should be found in the client's file.

- Company sales materials should not have any additions, deletions or modifications. For example, stickers updating information are improper unless provided by the company.

- The approval of agent-developed sales materials by one company does not extend to other companies' products. If an agent has approval from a company to use a piece of agent-developed sales material, it should be used only in conjunction with the sale of that company's products.

- All sales materials in the agent's possession, regardless of whether they are given to the client, should be the most up-to-date version available. This includes any illustration software on the agent's computer. Some companies include in their approval the date after which a piece may no longer be used without re-approval. The general agent or agency manager may wish to note this date and follow-up on it to be assured that outdated forms are no longer being used or that they have been submitted for re-approval. Other companies provide lists of updated or expired sales materials. When reviewing client files, the general agent or agency manager should determine whether the sales materials used were the most up-to-date version available at the time of the sale.

- The agent should be asked to provide for review any sales materials kept in his or her auto, home or any other location where he or she does business.

A copy of a completed and dated audit checklist provides appropriate documentation.

Some general agents and agency managers coordinate the purchase of or requests for sales materials for their agents. Keeping records of this process can help the general agent or agency manager to identify agents who may not be using company-approved sales materials. An agent who seems to be ordering or using less company sales materials than his or her sales would necessitate, may be using his or her own versions. Even if these are approved, the agent should be using company sales materials to provide documentation of product features and benefits.

Some general agents or agency managers maintain a database of all approved agent-, agency- or office-developed sales materials, which can be used to identify the expiration dates of sales materials and follow-up with agents monthly. Companies differ widely on how long their approval lasts. Some require annual re-approval; others provide unlimited approval for some sales materials. This can complicate the monitoring and re-approval process.

General agents or agency managers should also test all agency or office sales materials periodically to determine whether they are test most current version. Some companies provide printed listings of their approved, up-to-date sales materials; others provide them on their web sites.

You should check these listings to ensure that unapproved or outdated materials are not provided to agents. A copy of these listings should be kept in the agency or office compliance files as documentation. Because of the large volume of sales material available from companies, most general agents and agency managers do not develop their own database for tracking company sales material.

The general agent or agency manager should keep one copy of any agent-, agency- or office-approved sales material his or her agents use in the agency or office compliance files. When material becomes out-of-date, the date the expired sales materials were disposed of should be noted in the file to document what was used as well as that the other copies were destroyed. For company-provided sales materials, the company listings of expired or out-of-date sales materials are appropriate.

■ MONITORING PROPER DISCLOSURE

Why

Companies have found that a common theme in many client complaints is inadequate disclosure of policy or contract features, benefits and costs. For example, an agent who does not fully explain the surrender and withdrawal charges in an annuity may have to field numerous questions from clients who discover these charges when they attempt to take money out of their annuities. When client expectations are not met or clients discover surprises in how their products operate, they may lodge complaints against the agent. Failure to create realistic expectations about how insurance products function can lead to clients who are dissatisfied, frustrated and confused.

Most companies and regulators require full disclosure. Some companies require that a disclosure form be completed and provided to the client during the sale. Some states require that buyer's guides be provided. The NASD requires that a prospectus be provided as part of the sale of any registered product. In addition, numerous regulations require agents or companies to provide information on free look periods, complaint procedures, etc.

When

Proper disclosure should be reviewed for each sale. Each application should be reviewed to determine that the requisite disclosures were acknowledged by the agent and client for the company form and applications used.

Once a policy has been issued, policy delivery should be monitored to ensure the policy is provided to the client in a timely fashion and that the free look period appropriate for the state of issue was disclosed. Policy delivery is important because most states require that the policy contain a summary form that provides important policy disclosures and other disclosures required in the policy contract.

How

Companies document disclosure through different methods, including a:

- client acknowledgement that information was presented, e.g., a signature on the application that acknowledges that a prospectus was provided;

- copy of a signed company disclosure form; or

- signed delivery receipt.

Applications should be reviewed for the appropriate signatures acknowledging disclosure and properly completed, required company forms. The administrative staff should use a checklist for reviewing applications, in which the presence of required disclosure acknowledgements should be included. A copy of a completed and dated checklist should provide appropriate documentation.

Sometimes it is difficult to monitor disclosure unless the agency, office or company requires the agent to use a disclosure form. What takes place in the interview between the agent and the client often is unrecorded and therefore unknown to the general agent or agency manager. The general agent or agency manager should require the use of a disclosure form for all sales, even if the company whose product is being sold does not require one.*

If a company requires a delivery receipt, a review of the delivery log (which lists every policy delivery date and documents that policies were delivered) should be reviewed on a periodic basis. A delivery log provides appropriate documentation. Some company client surveys include information about delivery, and their reports should be reviewed.

A general agent or agency manager can ask the following questions to help identify agents with potential disclosure issues:

- **Which agents have greater than average delays in delivering policies or contracts?** Delays in delivery of a policy or contract may suggest that agents are reluctant to deliver the policy because they have not provided full disclosure of its features and benefits. For example, a life insurance policy may have been rated, which will lead to a different premium than was originally quoted.

- **Which agents do not use sales materials in their presentations?** Agents who rely on verbal explanations of policy or contract features, benefits and costs may overlook or forget to discuss some features and benefits.

- **Which agents do not request copies of prospectuses, buyer's guides or other sales materials from the agency, office or company?** Agents who do

---

* For an example of a disclosure form and an explanation of its use, see Dennis M. Groner, *Practical Compliance for Insurance Professionals* (LIMRA International: Hartford, CT, 2001).

not order required disclosure materials are not using them to provide proper disclosure.

- **Which agents generate significantly more client calls to administrative staff about how their policies operate?** This may suggest that the agent is not providing full disclosure of the product's operation.

- **Which agents sell large numbers of small policies or contracts?** Agents who have become comfortable in a market niche in which they sell the same small policy, for example, to fraternal members or members of the armed forces, may unintentionally be providing less than proper disclosure of features and benefits.

- **Are clients indicating that they are confused about their purchase?** Some companies use new client surveys, such as LIMRA's Customer Assurance Program (CAP) or one of their own design, to determine the client's level of understanding. Companies may provide information on specific agents or on the agency or office as a whole. Reviewing the survey results can identify whether clients are confused about their policy or contract's operation. Confusion about the purchase may suggest that proper disclosure did not take place during the sale.

- **Are the agents conducting policy delivery interviews?** Agents who do not conduct policy delivery interviews sometimes do not have the opportunity to provide enough disclosure.

The following are product or market issues that some general agents and agency managers monitor closely for potential disclosure issues. In most cases, general agents and agency managers meet periodically with agents who sell these products or operate in these markets to ensure that they are providing full disclosure:

- **Sales by new agents.** These should be reviewed for proper disclosure. In some cases, new agents may lack the experience, skill and knowledge to provide proper disclosure. General agents and agency managers can determine a new agent's level of knowledge and skill through role-play training and observing actual sales through joint work. They also can contact clients to determine whether full disclosure was provided.

- **Complex or large premium sales involving client advisors.** Clients may assume that all details about a product's features and benefits have been disclosed to their advisors, while advisors may assume the opposite. When several advisors, for example, CPAs and attorneys, are involved, one may assume that the other has been provided proper disclosure. Agents also may erroneously assume that full disclosure is not required because they are dealing with highly educated professionals. General agents and agency managers can interview agents involved in complex sales to determine whether they have provided proper disclosure.

- **Introduction of new products.** Agents need time to become familiar with the details of features and benefits. During the initial deployment of a new product, care should be exercised to ensure that proper disclosure takes place. General agents or agency managers can observe agent training or question agents to determine whether they are familiar with new products.

They also can contact the first clients who purchase these new products to determine whether full disclosure was provided.

- **Sales to seniors.** These may warrant additional scrutiny of disclosure. The general agent or agency manager may want to question agents who sell to seniors about whether or not the client understood the disclosures that were provided. If there are questions about the whether the senior client understood the disclosure, the agent or agency manager may suggest to the agent that the client have a family member or an advisor present to ensure that proper disclosure took place.

- **Cross sales of life insurance and property/casualty products.** These may require additional scrutiny of proper disclosure. Some companies offer a reduction in the premium of a property and casualty product, such as automobile insurance, if the client also owns a life insurance product with the same company. The agent should disclose that this reduced rate is available and that the purchase of life insurance is not required to purchase the auto policy. General agents and agency managers can contact a random sample of clients to determine whether proper disclosure was provided.

- **Sales of insurance products by agents in banks.** These require disclosure that the policies or contracts are not backed by any guarantees associated with bank deposit products. In addition, agents must be careful to disclose that life insurance offered to loan customers is not a requirement for the approval of the loan. General agents and agency managers of agents who work in banks can periodically observe how agents make sales and how proper disclosure is provided.

- **Work site marketing.** These also can require additional monitoring of disclosure. Whenever large numbers of small premium policies are sold, potential for less than proper disclosure exists because of an emphasis on concluding the sale quickly or the assumption that information was provided by a third party (e.g., a company representative) at an earlier meeting. General agents and agency managers can review the information given to clients, interview the company representatives and contact a random sample of clients to determine whether proper disclosure is being provided.

A general agent or agency manager can document that he or she has monitored these market or product issues by noting the date and result of the monitoring in the agency or office compliance file.

MONITORING PROPER COMPLETION OF APPLICATIONS AND FORMS

Why

The increase in the size and complexity of some companies' applications may give rise to errors in their completion. Administrative errors involving applications and forms can lead to potential compliance problems. For example, improperly completed forms may tempt agents or administrative staff to make changes on applications without obtaining new client or agent acknowledgment in the form of signatures or initials. Reviewing the completion of forms also can identify potential compliance or market conduct problems, e.g., improper signatures.

When

Every application and form should be reviewed before submission to a company. Early review can spot potential problems when they can be most easily resolved. Review of replacement and disclosure forms has been addressed already in this course. However, the complexity of some companies' applications provides ample additional areas for review.

How

The general agent or agency manager should request guidelines for completing applications from the companies with which with he or she has relationships. Company manuals often can provide valuable guidelines. With this as a basis, and with the help of the agency or office administrative staff, he or she should develop guidelines and checklists for reviewing applications. To streamline the review process, we recommend that a general checklist be developed that can be used for several companies' products.

Applications should be reviewed to determine whether they have been completed properly, signatures are appropriate and valid and all requirements and attachments are provided.

Agents and administrative staff should be trained in using the checklist. Rather than keep a separate checklist for each application, it is best to keep a log of all submitted applications, including the date the application was reviewed, the results of the review, the reviewer and his or her signature or initials acknowledging the review. This log should be maintained and reviewed periodically by the general agent or agency manager to ensure that it is being used appropriately.

The application log should be monitored by periodically selecting a random sample of reviewed applications and having another qualified person re-review them. This re-review should identify whether the applications are being reviewed on a timely and appropriate basis.

MONITORING MONEY LAUNDERING

Why

On October 26, 2001, the USA Patriot Act of 2001 took effect subjecting financial institutions and their agents and employees to stringent anti-money laundering requirements. This act built on earlier anti-money laundering regulations to expand the responsibilities of companies for detecting and preventing money laundering.

It is a Federal regulation (U.S. Code of Federal Regulations, Title 26, Section 60501 and Section 5331 of the Title 31 USC) that you must notify the IRS using its Form 8300 of any transaction involving $10,000 or more in currency or a cashier's check.

This includes an aggregate amount composed of traveler's checks, bank drafts, money orders, etc., paid over a 12-month period. It is illegal to aid in evading reporting cases of potential money laundering.

When

Agents should be made aware of company policies and procedures aimed at identifying potential instances of money laundering. Beginning in 2001, many companies have provided training in anti-money laundering. This training should be used. Every application should be reviewed prior to submission to a company. However, the best time to spot a potential money laundering situation is during the sale.

How

The general agent and agency manager through his or her administrative staff should routinely monitor all applications to identify potential instances. He or she should request guidelines for screening applications or sales for potential money laundering from the companies with which he or she has a relationship. Company manuals sometimes provide such guidelines. With this as a basis, and with the help of the agency or office administrative staff, he or she should develop guidelines and checklists for reviewing applications.

When reviewing applications or sales activity, the following are some signs that a potential money laundering situation may be occurring. These signs can be used along with any company suggested indicators to develop a checklist that the general agent's and agency manager's staff can use to screen applications.

Upon identifying a potential money laundering situation, the general agent and agency manager should immediately contact the agent and obtain additional information to confirm or deny his or her suspicions. If it appears that this is a potential case of money laundering, the case should be immediately reported to the company whose product is being sold. Company guidelines should be followed to identify the appropriate contact. Together with the company, a strategy for taking action should be developed.

The following are some signals or signs that a potential sale may involve money laundering.

- The client wants to pay premiums in cash, traveler's checks, postal money orders, etc.

- The client pays the premium with a third-party check and the relationship between the client and the third party is unclear.

- The client is not concerned about investment returns, fees, surrender costs, etc.

- Payment for the policy involves a complicated transfer of funds from several sources.

- The client uses wire transfers to move large amounts of money to or from foreign countries.

- The client uses a mailing address that is a post office box or outside the country.

- The agent is making the sale to a client in another state and may have only briefly met the client.

- The product chosen does not require a medical examination, credit data, etc.

- The agent has not conducted a need analysis.

- The client's reason for buying the product is unclear or unrelated to the client's apparent financial situation, means or needs.

- The client is reluctant to provide personal information or provides incorrect, incomplete or misleading information.

- There is no pre-existing relationship between the agent, the client or a third party, i.e., a stranger approaches the agent regarding the sale.

- The client knows the product he or she wishes to purchase and is unwilling to discuss additional products or needs.

- The client wishes to purchase several single-payment products for family members or wishes to purchase several single-payment products over a 12-month period.

- The agent has a number of "not takens" on policies that include the initial premium or investment with the application. This is one way to launder cash without having to pay any surrender charges later on.

MONITORING LICENSING

Why

States require that all individuals who solicit the sale of insurance products or are compensated based on the sale of insurance products be properly licensed. The NASDR requires that only properly registered representatives of broker-dealers may sell registered products or receive compensation from the sale of registered products. General agents and agency managers should monitor the license status of their agents and administrative staff to avoid potential compliance problems.

When

The general agent or agency manager should make certain before the solicitation or sale of any insurance product that the individual selling the products properly licensed and appointed, if required by state regulation. In addition, states require that licensed agents maintain their licenses through meeting continuing education requirements and paying license renewal fees. The NASD also requires that registered representatives meet continuing education requirements. General agents and agency managers also should monitor their licensed agents and registered representatives to ensure that they maintain their licenses in good standing.*

How

There are four steps in monitoring and supervising licensing:

1. Does the agent or the administrative staff person have the proper license or registration before soliciting the sale of an insurance product?

2. Does the administrative person who may be in contact with clients have the proper NASD registration to provide the support expected?

3. Is the agent or administrative staff person properly appointed by the company whose product is being solicited before the solicitation?

4. Is the agent or administrative staff person's license or registration up-to-date, i.e., have all fees been paid and have continuing education requirements been met?

Licensing requirements depend on state and NASDR regulations. The general agent or agency manager should identify the specific requirements for each state in which his or her agents do business, because state regulations governing licensing and appointment vary and state license requirements depend on the client's state of residence. This information should be available from the companies with which the general agent or agency manager has a relationship.

Most companies review agent license status as part of the application process, and most general agents and agency managers rely on this review to ensure that the agent has the proper license. Some general agents and agency managers include questions about license status in the checklist or guidelines used to screen applications for completeness and accuracy.

A related concern arises when an agent solicits business from residents of a state in which he or she does not currently have a license. This often is a problem in areas where there are several contiguous states in which the agent can easily do business, e.g., New Jersey, New York and Connecticut. The agent should have the proper license and appointment status before actively soliciting business in a state. The general agent or agency manager should review the activity of a new, inexperienced or unlicensed agent or staff associate to ensure that he or she is prospecting for business in the state in which licensing requirements are met. When hiring agents, general agents or agency managers should obtain copies of all their licenses during the selection process. This information can be included in the checklist or guidelines used to screen applications for completeness and accuracy.

General agents and agency managers should monitor the sales-related activity of any administrative staff to be assured that they are properly licensed for the

---

* For additional information on general licensing requirements, see Dennis M. Groner, *Practical Compliance for Insurance Professionals* (LIMRA International: Hartford, CT, 2001).

activities in which they participate. This is especially important for administrative staff that interact with clients regarding registered products. Some administrative staff may inadvertently provide investment-related advice to clients. For example, a client asks questions over the telephone regarding other investment options in a variable annuity they own. In an effort to help, the staff member may provide information on the various options, their performance, their popularity among other clients, etc. Providing this advice, even on a service basis, may require that the administrative staff be registered.

Many general agents or agency managers monitor agent and administrative staff license status annually or semi-annually by conducting a review, examination or audit of the agent's practice. If this is one of the ways the general agent or agency manager monitors license status, he or she should include the review questions in any guidelines used and should file the date and results of the review. Maintain this information with copies of the agent or staff associate's licenses in compliance files.

Commissions from insurance sales should be paid only to individuals who are properly licensed. Splitting commissions on a formal or informal basis between agents, only one of whom is properly licensed or registered, is improper and should be monitored by the general agent or agency manager.

Most companies provide reports on commissions. Usually, these reports can be used to identify whether commissions have been split. Although most companies exercise care in providing split commissions, the general agent and agency manager should check these commission statements and reports for indications of improper split commissions.

Some agents may provide a bonus based on a sale to another agent or administrative staff person which may be, in essence, a split commission without notifying the company whose product was sold. General agents and agency managers sometimes find this difficult to monitor, because it is a private transaction between the agent and another individual. Unless the general agent and agency manager has access to the agent's business accounting records, it may not be apparent that this type of split has taken place. However, the general agent and agency manager still should include this subject in his or her semi-annual or annual review, examination or audit of the agent's practice. A review question in any guidelines he or she uses, the date and results of the review are appropriate documentation. Maintain this information with copies of the agent or staff associate's licenses.

License Renewals

The general agent or agency manager also should confirm that the agent and administrative staff person's licenses are up-to-date. To do this, he or she should monitor that all fees have been paid, all continuing education requirements have been met and the proper paperwork has been submitted to the state. In most cases, the company or the broker-dealer monitors the license status of registered representatives and handles the required documentation.

One way to monitor license status is to create a calendar that lists when each agent or staff associate must renew his or her license. The general agent or agency manager then can follow-up 60 days before the deadline to determine whether they are making progress in doing so. Some general agents and agency managers include time in their calendars for—and periodically remind agents and administrative staff about—the need to meet their continuing education requirements.

A calendar that lists all agent renewal dates or examples of notices to agents to renew their licenses should be appropriate documentation that the general agent or agency manager has monitored license renewal status.

■ GENERAL INDICATORS OF POTENTIAL MARKET CONDUCT AND COMPLIANCE PROBLEMS

There are some general indicators of potential market conduct and compliance problems to which general agents and agency managers should be sensitive. The following are signs that there may be a problem. Spotting these signs early and closely supervising an agent, administrative staff member or member of management may help stop a problem before it becomes a serious infraction of company rules and state or NASDR regulations and laws. Bearing this in mind, the general agent and agency manager should never jump to conclusions based on these indicators—they simply indicate the possibility of a problem:

- Signs of possible financial problems:

    - requests to borrow money from agents, managers or administrative staff members;

    - requests for commission, salary or expense advances;

    - unexpected financial obligations (e.g., personal or family medical bills);

    - calls by creditors and notification of wage garnishment;

    - changes in lifestyle or spending habits that do not correlate with income; or

    - gambling losses.

- Signs of possible personal problems:

    - dramatic changes in personality or attitudes (e.g., evasive, belligerent or insubordinate);

    - marital or family problems;

    - personal or family member substance abuse problems;

    - repeated telephone calls from family members during the day; or

    - inappropriate or ineffective work habits (e.g., working at odd hours, disorganization, failure to be present for important meetings, complaints from clients about missed meetings).

- Other signs of possible problems:

  - low morale;

  - defensiveness when questioned;

  - unusually close business relationships with clients involving outside business interests;

  - spending significant time on outside business interests while in the agency or office;

  - unfounded criticism of agency management, company policies or other agents;

  - inconsistent sales activity or production, or dramatic changes in sales activity or production;

  - large numbers of calls from clients, which are not returned on a timely basis; or

  - long absences from work without notice.

ERRORS TO AVOID IN SUPERVISING COMPLIANCE AND MARKET CONDUCT

There are some classic or common errors that general agents and agency managers should avoid when supervising market conduct and compliance:

- **Failing to recognize the impact of a potentially improper sale.** It does not take much to create a potential market conduct problem. Something as simple as an improper explanation of the costs and benefits of a product or the failure to disclose important information can lead to big problems. Every sale, therefore, must be scrutinized. Time pressures and the need to keep business moving, however, can make it difficult to take a close look at every sale. In addition, sometimes managers may be blind to small problems. For example, a manager may be rooting for an agent to pull out of a slump and miss signs that a sale has features that should be setting off market conduct alarms. Managers must pay attention to every sale, even if it is small and routine and an agent assures the manager that everything is, "okay despite some loose ends," with the sale. Because every sale could be a potential market conduct problem, every sale deserves careful scrutiny. A manager cannot afford to ignore any sale, no matter how small or simple, for warning signals.

- **Excusing top performers from close supervision.** It is natural for a general agent or agency manager to unconsciously excuse the potential problems of a top performer because that agent has earned respect for outstanding contributions over the years. General agents and agency managers sometimes avoid asking the tough questions for fear of alienating their top agents. In some cases, they may rely on talking with the agent's administrative staff people, who may not know the details well enough to help the general agent or agency manager determine whether action must be taken. The size of the sale and its potential override sometimes blinds general agents and agency managers to potential problems. General agents and agency managers should guard against the tendency to excuse top performers and instead treat them like any other agent when it comes to supervising compliance and market conduct.

- **Blaming agents instead of helping them improve their performance.** Once burned by a compliance or market conduct problem, some general agents and agency managers become so punitive that they drive agents and their staff underground with potential problems and questions. General agents and agency managers must be careful not to ignore common sense in taking a stand on compliance and market conduct. General agents and agency managers who have a take-no-prisoners approach to market conduct will be the last to know if there is a potential problem. Agents and their administrative staff are likely to approach the general agent or agency manager with a potential problem if they know they will get a full and fair hearing rather than an immediate reprimand. Using potential problems as a learning experience is the best strategy for keeping lines of communication open. General agents and agency managers need to avoid the habit of always telling agents what not to do and instead communicate how to do it properly.

- **Practicing herd management.** General agents and agency managers sometimes fail to pay attention to the differences between the practices, markets and personalities of individual agents in their supervision. They may ignore the differences in markets, yet markets require different sensitivities to market conduct issues, e.g., sales to seniors. They may need to pay more attention to the new member of the sales team, who may not be as knowledgeable about company procedures even though they are highly experienced. Agents who have a tendency to come on too strong should be more carefully supervised to ensure they are not creating potential problems. Agents who sometimes are sloppy in taking care of details also need additional help. General agents and agency managers should tailor their supervision and monitoring to each agent's style, personality and market.

- **Making compliance supervision an add on to other activities rather than a stand-alone function.** Most general agents and agency managers are very busy, and unless their priorities are straight, they can end up devoting too little time and attention to compliance and market conduct. Some general agents and agency managers make supervising compliance and market conduct a good thing to do—rather than a required thing to do—that gets rescheduled over and over again. For example, they may try to combine reviewing compliance reports with reviewing performance reports and end up not spending enough time on the former. Or they may include reviewing compliance issues in their performance review meetings with individuals they have delegated compliance monitoring to and never get to the compliance part of the agenda. In the long run, supervising compliance and market conduct will suffer from a lack of continuous attention.

- **Assuming that the company is responsible.** Some general agents and agency managers assume that a company's home office will catch unsuitable sales, hidden replacements and other potential compliance and market conduct problems. They may not give careful scrutiny at the agency level because they have confidence in home office auditing and supervision.

Sometimes this confidence is misplaced because even when the home office supervises compliance well, it often occurs so long after the problem that damage has already been done. General agents and agency managers are closer to the actual sale and have a better chance to head-off potential problems before they grow unmanageable. General agents and agency managers always should assume that they are responsible and seek ways to reduce the risk that comes with that responsibility.

- **Delegating too much responsibility for compliance to others.** General agents and agency managers can and should delegate some of their compliance and market conduct responsibilities to their administrative staff. It is easy, however, to delegate too much responsibility to administrative staff members who have too little training, experience and authority. General agents and agency managers sometimes realize this error only when confronted by the failure to identify and act on a potential compliance or market conduct problem. General agents and agency managers who are registered principals are more limited in what they can delegate because of NASD requirements, but all general agents and agency managers should carefully identify those tasks that can be delegated, provide their staff with the proper training to accomplish them and then closely supervise how those tasks are carried out. Delegation is rarely an adequate defense against alleged failure to carry out supervisory responsibility. In the final analysis, the general agent or agency manager ultimately is responsible.

■ HOW TO EFFECTIVELY IMPLEMENT ENHANCEMENTS TO SUPERVISORY SYSTEMS

Once a general agent or agency manager has reviewed his or her current supervisory system and identified ways to enhance it, he or she is faced with the task of effectively implementing those enhancements. This is the same task faced when implementing changes or enhancements in monitoring mandated by the companies with which he or she has a relationship. For some general agents or agency managers, implementing change can be a significant obstacle.

Why Some Agents Resist Monitoring and Supervision

To highly ethical insurance professionals, compliance rules and regulations seem to be the common sense way of conducting their practice. Some, however, chafe at the control and supervision general agents, agency managers and companies exercise over their activities. Perhaps some agents have an entrepreneurial, independent spirit that does not respond well to outside controls. Others resist because they do not understand that effective monitoring and supervision is valuable to them. Others fear that supervision and monitoring of their sales processes may lead to lost sales because of additional requirements or time delays. Agent and administrative staff resistance to change sometimes is a barrier that a general agent or agency manager must overcome to provide effective monitoring and supervision.

When developing enhancements to supervisory systems, general agents and agency managers should remember that some agents might resist their efforts at monitoring and supervision. As they begin the process of enhancing their supervisory system, general agents and agency managers should keep in mind that implementing potential enhancements successfully is an important key to making supervision and monitoring successful.

Tips on Implementing Enhancements

General agents and agency managers may need to do the following as part of their process of implementing new monitoring and supervisory procedures:

- Explain to each agent and administrative staff person that monitoring and supervision can help avoid potential compliance problems.

- Provide agents with examples of how other agents who resisted monitoring and supervision have paid a price for it.

- Provide monitoring and supervision as a service that can help the agent reduce his or her potential liability for compliance and market conduct errors.

- Explain to the agent that the supervisory role of the general agent or agency manager is required by companies to meet the their responsibility to regulators.

- Demonstrate his or her supervisory role by taking action on agents that do not submit to supervision, such as terminating their contracts.

- Involve agents and administrative staff in the process of enhancing current monitoring and supervisory procedures so that they have input on the design of the enhancements.

- Educate agents about their supervisory responsibility for administrative staff as a way to help them understand the general agent and agency manager's responsibility for them.

- Ask companies for information to help educate agents and administrative staff on supervisory responsibilities.

- Form an agent and administrative staff committee to provide counsel to the general agent and agency manager in how to take action in situations where individuals do not follow procedures.

- Involve agents and administrative staff in planning for the implementation of compliance initiatives, such as the annual meeting.

- Ask agents and administrative staff to participate in the process of identifying compliance and market conduct roadblocks in agency or office procedures and developing solutions for removing them.

- Do not try to implement too many enhancements at once. Sometimes it is effective to develop a plan for implementing enhancements that goes from the easiest and least disruptive to the most difficult and disruptive so that agents and administrative staff can gain experience in making changes.

- Share the details of the system with everyone involved. Though the specific data might be confidential, the system and how it operates should be public knowledge.

- Provide regular feedback to agents on what is being monitored and the results of the monitoring. Often this will be praise that they are doing a good job of being in compliance and providing proper market conduct.

In some cases, resistance is caused by a lack of understanding and a fear of the unknown. The more agents and administrative staff know about what the general agent and agency manager and the companies they represent plan to do and why it is necessary, the easier it will be for them to adapt to any of the new procedures and processes that are implemented. This requires ongoing communication throughout the identification, design and development of enhancements.

General agents and agency managers meet resistance if they make monitoring and supervision an onerous, difficult process to live with. It is a good strategy to involve agents and administrative staff members in making the monitoring procedures as simple and easy to follow as possible. Their involvement will improve the final system and ensure that they have ownership in it. Ensure that monitoring systems work before implementing them on a widespread basis. Pilot test and refine them by using them with one or two agents before implementing them full scale.

6

Taking Corrective Action on Potential Compliance and Market Conduct Issues

WHY MUST THE GENERAL AGENT OR AGENCY MANAGER TAKE CORRECTIVE ACTION?

Once a potential compliance issue is identified, the general agent or agency manager should take timely action to resolve it. Ignoring a known compliance or market conduct problem is a serious error in judgement. Not taking timely, appropriate action can give the impression that the manager condones or was a party to the improper action.

General agents and agency managers must be prepared to take action on any potential infractions or improprieties related to regulator or company rules, policies and procedures. They also must be prepared to take action on any infractions of the agency or office ethics statement and all potential improprieties in the areas they monitor and supervise. Monitoring and supervision without taking action implies a lack of concern and is an important part of alleged failure to supervise. It also sends a subtle signal to the agency or office personnel that though the general agent or agency manager claims to be concerned about proper compliance and market conduct, that concern is not backed up with concrete action. This will undermine efforts to develop agency and office commitment to standards.

Because the timing of monitoring and supervision is a function of the compliance issue being monitored, its importance and the data used to identify potential compliance issues, general agents and agency managers may need to take action on an ongoing basis. They must be prepared with a process that allows them to carry out their responsibility in a timely and appropriate manner. This process also should be consistent, fair, equitable and able to stand up to the scrutiny of a company or regulator.

WHICH ISSUES SHOULD BE HANDLED BY A GENERAL AGENT OR AGENCY MANAGER?

Some companies require the general agent or agency manager to contact them if he or she has identified any misconduct. This requirement may be in the contract or in a company policy or procedure manual. Other companies require an agent, administrative staff member or manager associated with the company to report any suspected violations of company policy. This policy may be in the company's ethics statement, contract or description of general policies and procedures. Some companies provide a toll-free number to report suspected violations of company policy.

The general agent or agency manager should know whether company policy obligates him or her to contact the company and report potential misconduct or failure to follow company procedures. Sometimes it is unclear, however, whether a particular situation warrants contacting a company to report possible misconduct or failure to follow company policies and procedures. This is especially true when a general agent or agency manager has a supervisory system that provides an early warning of potential problems. For example, in the following situations, there may be uncertainty whether a situation must be reported:

- A general agent or agency manager identifies a potentially unsuitable sale before the application is submitted to a company and has the agent meet with the client again and select a more suitable one.

- A general agent or agency manager determines that the agent may not have provided proper disclosure and remedies the situation by having the agent provide proper disclosure at the time of policy delivery.

- A general agent or agency manager identifies a signature on an application that may not be appropriate and has the agent get a new, appropriately signed application.

- A general agent or agency manager determines that an administrative staff person was engaged in activities defined as soliciting insurance without having a license and requires that the person obtain a license before having any further client contact.

Some instances of misconduct or failure to follow company procedures clearly call for immediate and serious action by a company, e.g., forgery, theft of funds, misrepresentation, repeated improper conduct and disguising replacements.

However, general agents and agency managers often find themselves in a quandary about what must be reported to a company and the actions they can take on a local level. This is especially true when a failure to follow company procedures is not directly related to regulations. For example, if the agent does not maintain files according to company policy or does not follow company procedures when delivering a policy but violates no law or regulation, general agents and agency managers question whether they must report the agent to the company or can take action on their own. For general agents or agency managers with relationships with many different companies, this can pose an even greater problem, because each company's standards may differ.

There are no easy answers to these questions. One strategy would be to contact the company and ask in general terms if a particular situation must be reported and use that as a basis for determining how to proceed. A more conservative strategy would be to report any violation of company policy and procedure. Though this can protect the general agent or agency manager from potential liability for the misconduct or violation of company policy, it may create an unhealthy atmosphere in an agency or office.

Another issue is which companies need to be notified. Must the general agent and agency manager contact all of the companies the agent has a relationship with or only the one whose product is involved in the potential misconduct? For example, if the general agent or agency manager identifies that the agent has engaged in falsifying information on an application, he or she may have to notify all of the companies with which the agent has a relationship and not just the one whose application was involved. Failure to do so may increase the risk of being held liable for failing to notify a company of a potential problem with the agent. However, if the misconduct involves a company policy, it may not need to be shared with other companies. For example, some companies require the agent to deliver the policy to the client and obtain a delivery receipt, while others do not. If the agent fails to obtain a delivery receipt for a company that requires it, the general agent or agency manager need not report the infraction to the other companies.

Finally, if the general agent or agency manager is a registered principal with supervisory responsibility over the agent, his or her options are even more limited. Registered principals have even less freedom to take independent action on a registered representative's potential misconduct because they are required to notify their broker-dealer. This typically is detailed in their supervisory guidelines. Failure to do so can have serious repercussions.

HOW SHOULD A GENERAL AGENT OR AGENCY MANAGER TAKE CORRECTIVE ACTION ON POSSIBLE COMPLIANCE ISSUES?

A general agent or agency manager should ask the following questions regarding each possible instance of misconduct or failure to follow company procedures before deciding on a specific course of action:

- What are the specific policies, procedures or regulations that may have been violated?

- Does the general agent or agency manager have enough facts regarding the possible misconduct or failure to follow company procedures?

- How can the investigation of this situation be kept confidential?

- Why did the agent or administrative staff person act in a possibly improper way?

- Are there any extenuating circumstances?

- What are the consequences of the possible misconduct or failure to follow company procedures for the client, the company and the agent?

- What could be done to make the situation better?

- Is this an isolated instance or part of an ongoing pattern of misconduct or failure to follow company procedures?

- Which other instances of possible misconduct or failures to follow company procedures may be associated with the one being examined?

- What must be documented to comply with company policies and procedures?

- Which companies should be contacted?

The key to taking action effectively is to have as much information as possible before confronting an agent and to have examined all aspects of the situation before deciding what to do. This requires detailed investigation of situation and facts, but the general agent or agency manager does not have unlimited time to conduct an investigation. Long, drawn-out investigations may look like attempts to avoid taking action. Also, additional instances of possible misconduct may be occurring while investigations are taking place.

Any investigations of possible improprieties or market conduct problems should be documented carefully. Notes from interviews with clients and agents, sample reports, copies of applications, evidence from policy files, etc., should be included in the documentation.

Any investigation should be conducted in the most discreet and confidential manner possible. Any discussions with clients, administrative staff members or other agents should be handled with the utmost care.

HOW SHOULD A GENERAL AGENT OR AGENCY MANAGER HANDLE COMPANY-INSTIGATED INVESTIGATIONS?

General agents and agency managers must be especially careful of potential improprieties and market conduct problems identified by companies themselves. Companies' home office staff are far removed from the actual sale and must use data that can be open to interpretation. For example, some companies may contact new clients by mail or telephone to ask if a needs analysis was performed or a replacement occurred. This is a valuable method of collecting data on potential suitability problems or hidden replacements. When the general agent or agency manager follows up with the client, however, he or she often learns that the alleged problem was based on miscommunication or misinterpretation by the client or the company. Sometimes, the further away the investigator is from the actual sale, the more care must be taken to determine whether a potential market conduct or compliance problem actually occurred.

Companies track transactions that can indicate hidden replacements. Although a lapse of a current policy, contract or loan six months after a new policy is sold may appear suspicious, an investigation is needed before accusing anyone of misconduct. General agents and agency managers often discover that what appears to be misconduct is not.

Whenever a general agent or agency manager is asked to conduct a company-requested investigation of a potential impropriety or market conduct problem, he or she should take the request seriously and carry out a timely and complete investigation. Depending on the severity of the potential problem, he or she may not want to delegate any part of the investigation to others. Confidentiality is critical. He or she often will be asked to document the investigation and provide a letter to the company with the findings. Some companies use forms as a template for the documentation and report.

General agents and agency managers should exercise care when completing documentation or reports of investigations. The report should be based on collected evidence and not on suspicions, suppositions or theories. Documented reports that are poorly written, jump to conclusions or are not based on sufficient facts may be used against you should legal proceedings occur.

WHICH CORRECTIVE ACTIONS SHOULD BE TAKEN?

Sadly, agents, administrative staff and managers sometimes make mistakes that require corrective action. The purposes of corrective actions are to:

- stop the continued improprieties;

- educate those involved;

- resolve problems with a client who has been treated improperly;

- allow the general agent or agency manager and company to assign responsibility for the impropriety and develop procedures to avoid future occurrences;

- serve as a basis for ongoing supervision and monitoring;

- discipline individuals based on the severity and frequency of their improprieties;

- provide regulators with information regarding improper actions; and

- demonstrate to others in the agency and office that improper conduct will not be tolerated.

The decision-making process used to determine which corrective action is most appropriate should be tailored to the severity of the impropriety or market conduct error and its frequency. A single mistake may require one type of corrective action; repeated mistakes may require another.

The standards for choosing a corrective action should be consistent, fair and equitable. Failure to do so can lead to claims that the general agent or agency manager discriminated against the agent, administrative staff member or manager, which can lead to additional legal and human resources problems.

Companies often have discipline matrices to ensure a documented, equitable process for determining corrective action. The following is an example of such a matrix. This matrix is provided for illustrative purposes only.

Sample Corrective Action Matrix			
Seriousness of Misconduct	*Frequency of Misconduct*		
	First Instance	*Second Instance*	*Third+ Instance*
Level 1: Failure to follow administrative procedures, negative audit results, improperly completed applications, etc.	Development action plan and quarterly supervisory follow-up for 6 months	Warning letter, development plan and quarterly supervisory follow-up for 12 months	Selling privileges suspended for 6 months to termination, depending on the number of repeated instances
Level 2: Improper suitability, improper disclosure, failure to provide replacement forms on a timely basis	Warning letter, development plan and quarterly supervisory follow-up for 2 months	Selling privileges suspended for 6 months, followed by quarterly supervisory follow-up for 12 months	Termination
Level 3: Improper or hidden replacements, failure to notify the company of complaints, etc.	Fine not to exceed $1,000, selling privileges suspended for 6 months, followed by quarterly supervisory follow-up for 12 months	Termination	
Level 4: Misuse or theft or client of company funds, forgery, etc.	Termination		

General agents and agency managers may want to obtain sample matrices from companies they have a relationship with and develop a matrix to use in their agencies.

The typical range of corrective actions is:

- coaching and counseling with no formal development plan;
- a formal development plan that requires education and additional supervision;
- fines, restrictions and sanctions (e.g., suspension of privileges or probation); or
- termination.

Each of these corrective actions can be adapted to the specific circumstances of an agency, office or company.

HOW SHOULD THE GENERAL AGENT OR AGENCY MANAGER MAKE CERTAIN THE MISTAKE IS NOT REPEATED?

One of most important purposes of corrective action is to educate agents, administrative staff and managers because most improprieties and market conduct problems result from ignorance or an error in judgement. If everyone who ever made a mistake or committed an error of judgement was terminated, many agencies and offices would be empty.

The simplest and most direct way to help a person who has made a mistake is to provide coaching and counseling. Many simple and less serious administrative errors, improprieties or market conduct problems can be resolved through a discussion aimed at helping the person understand the importance of following procedures properly. Though no formal written development plan need be created, the general agent or agency manager should document that a discussion was held on the issue.

The key to an effective coaching and counseling session on market conduct is to accomplish the following:

- Clearly identify the improper behavior or conduct or error.

- Specify what was done improperly and what would have been the correct or proper behavior to use.

- Obtain an admission of responsibility for the improper behavior.

- Describe the severity of the improper behavior and why it was improper.

- Determine why the improper behavior occurred.

- Provide examples of how to avoid the improper behavior in the future.

- Identify the negative consequences of future improper behavior.

- Obtain a commitment from the agent, administrative staff person or manager not to repeat the improper behavior.

- Identify how the general agent or agency manager will help out by following up to prevent future improper behavior, provide additional resources, coaching, etc.

If the severity or frequency of the improper conduct requires a formal training or development plan, the same coaching process can be used. However, the greater the severity, the more the general agent or agency manager should emphasize the negative consequences of future improprieties. The meeting's tone should be serious and the warning explicit.

A formal training or development plan is one way for the general agent, agency manager or company to ensure that identified misconduct or improprieties are documented, corrected and supervised. A formal plan helps ensure that reasonable effort was made to deal with the improprieties. It gives the agent, administrative staff person or manager the opportunity to remedy deficiencies and demonstrate proper conduct.

Both parties should work together to develop the specifics of the plan to tailor it to the agent's market, procedures and needs. This can be done in a preliminary meeting, following which the general agent or agency manager should put the plan in writing and schedule a second meeting at which the plan can be discussed and agreed to by the agent.

Many plans include the following:

- a description of the improper behavior, conduct or error;

- the reasons why the improper behavior occurred;

- the agent's admission that he or she acted improperly;

- the steps the agent will take to keep from committing the improper behavior in the future;

- the training, education and resources that general agent or agency manager will provide to help the agent avoid improper actions in the future;

- a description of the specific techniques, tools and procedures the agent is required to use or follow;

- specific behavior or conduct the agent is prohibited from engaging in;

- a description of the periodic reporting, monitoring or supervision that the general agent, agency manager or his or her designee will carry out;

- the time period the plan will be in effect;

- the standards that will be used to determine whether the plan has been accomplished successfully;

- a description of the potential consequences if the plan is not completed; and

- the agent and general agent or agency manager's signature and the date.

The agent should receive a copy of the plan. The general agent or agency manager should file a copy of the plan in the agent's personnel file and the agency or office compliance file. In some cases, a copy of the plan must be provided to the company whose products were involved in the specific impropriety or misconduct. This is especially true when a company has initiated the investigation. In some cases, the general agent or agency manager may be required to notify several companies.

WHAT IF THE EMPLOYEE MUST BE TERMINATED?

Some misconduct is so serious that it requires termination of the employee or the relationship between an employee and one or more companies. These situations are not only difficult, but require seriously attention to detail, procedures and regulations

Termination procedures for individuals with contracts with a company or general agent and agency manager sometimes differ from procedures for individuals who have no contract, such as administrative staff. This discussion of termination procedures will focus only on agent terminations. The general agent or agency manager should contact a legal advisor regarding termination procedures for noncontract employees or staff.

Once the general agent, agency manager or company decides to sever relations with an agent, it is important to handle the termination with care, consistency and confidentiality. Many company contracts give the general agent or agency manager the right to terminate the agent's contractual relationship by providing some period of notice, e.g., 30 days. In addition, companies also retain the right to terminate an agent. Some contracts give a company an immediate right of termination if the agent breaches the contract. Some general agent and agency manager contracts also provide this right.

It is important to review the relevant contracts carefully to structure the termination process correctly. Even when a company initiates the termination process, general agents and agency managers often are required to carry out the process. In most cases, before initiating termination, the general agent or agency manager should consult with the company whose contract is being severed. In some cases, the contract may not allow the general agent or agency manager to sever the agent's relationship with the company. In this case, the general agent or agency manager should seek legal advice regarding his or her options.

In most cases, only a broker-dealer may sever the contract between the registered representatives and the broker-dealer. When terminating registered representatives, the general agent or agency manager should work closely with the broker-dealer to determine the proper procedures to follow.

The following are some general guidelines and ideas to consider when handling terminations:

- seek company or legal advice before initiating termination;
- all terminations should be documented fully before informing the agent;
- all terminations should be planned before informing the agent;
- identify the general agent or agency manager's rights to client information, file and equipment retention, etc.;
- determine whether and how clients will be transferred to a new agent;
- identify compensation issues regarding pending business, charge backs, etc.;

- never begin termination procedures based on emotion or a gut-level reaction;

- determine whether termination need be limited only to the agent;

- the agent should receive a letter from the general agent, agency manager or company formally notifying him or her of termination and the terms and condition of the termination, including any communication to regulators (e.g., whether the broker-dealer will be submitting a Form U5 to the NASD or alerting a state regulator);

- identify security issues and how they will be handled (e.g., building, agency or office keys, agency or office general files, stores, personal safety of agency or office personnel, including the general agent and agency manager);

- develop a process for transferring clients either to a new agent or an administrative staff member, including how the clients will be contacted and informed of their new relationship; and

- develop a strategy to communicate to the rest of the agency or office the termination and its circumstances.

The general agent or agency manager should document the process used to terminate an agent in case questions arise afterwards. It is prudent to discuss with the company, agency or office legal counsel how best to document the termination process.

After termination, it is wise to conduct an inventory of the agent's files, company records, etc. Even if a prior audit or investigation involved an examination of files and records, the general agent or agency manager still should conduct an inventory and document the results of the examination. The inventory should verify that required records and files were not taken. It also should seek to identify potential areas of complaints or problems, including:

- blank forms with signatures;

- sample or practice client signatures;

- copies of client forms intended for clients' possession;

- undelivered policies or client information; or

- written or verbal evidence of complaints.

If client files contain any of the above materials, these clients should be contacted by a newly assigned agent or administrative staff person as soon as possible. If a potential problem surfaces, the general agent or agency manager should review the problem promptly and be involved in contacting and meeting with the client. The company whose product is involved should be contacted and provided with all pertinent details.

The general agent or agency manager should make and retain a backup copy of the agent's computer files. This provides a record that can be referred to if questions arise and also can assist any agents or administrative staff members assigned the former agent's clients.

All recovered client files should be retained by the agency or office. The new agent or administrative person responsible for contacting the client should receive the client file. He or she should be told to maintain the original file and also to begin a new file to identify which actions took place after the former agent was terminated. Any documents used from the original file should be copied for use in the new file and dated.

TIPS ON TAKING ACTION

The following are some suggestions or ideas to use when considering taking action:

- Investigate the issue to ensure that any suspicions of improper conduct are well founded before discussing the potential issue with the agent. If the potential misconduct or failure to follow company procedures was identified by someone else, such as an administrative staff person, ask to see the basis for the suspicion and discuss the issue.

- When a potential impropriety, instance of misconduct or failure to follow company procedures is identified by another member of the agency, e.g., a member of the administrative staff—sometimes called a whistleblower—carefully maintain the confidential nature of the allegation. People in the agency must feel that they can approach the general agent or agency manager with their concerns and receive acceptance, openness and objectivity. Even if the allegation is mistaken or unfounded, the general agent or agency manager should avoid criticizing the individual who shared his or her concern. The general agent or agency manager should be familiar with the policies of the companies with which he or she has a relationship. This can potentially be a complicated situation if the whistleblower also was involved in the impropriety, such as an administrative staff member who helped the agent carry out improper practices.

- Check the reliability and accuracy of any data or information used to identify the potential compliance issue, e.g., reports from companies on lapses. Be certain that the implications of the data are clear.

- Base your evaluation of the situation on as much data as possible. Try to paint as clear a picture of the situation or issue and how it happened.

- Maintain confidentiality of any agents suspected of improper conduct and of the subsequent investigation.

- Document what has been learned and the data or information used, and maintain copies of reports, notes from interviews, etc.

- Do not procrastinate or drag out your investigation of the situation. Conducting an overly long review could indicate an unwillingness to take action. If a serious impropriety has taken place, consider immediately taking action to stop the impropriety.

- Review company policies and procedures to determine how the company treats the situation or issue. Know the regulations that were violated or the company policies that were not followed. Should any extenuating circumstances be taken into account?

- Determine whether more than one company must be alerted to the situation.

- Present what has been learned to the agent as a hypothesis and ask for an explanation. Avoid accusing the agent of misconduct or impropriety until hearing his or her side of the story. Depending on the severity of the compliance situation or issue, it may be wise to require the agent's explanation in writing.

- An agent may dispute the evaluation of the situation. This is why the general agent or agency manager should have as much research as possible to support the hypothesis that a potential compliance situation or issue has occurred.

- If the agent does not accept the interpretation of the data, offer to have a third party, such as the company that may be involved, review the data.

- If the general agent or agency manager and the agent can resolve the situation or issue without contacting the company, the agent should be counseled on the issue, educated on the proper procedure and given a plan created to correct the situation.

- If the agent blames a member of his or her administrative staff for the impropriety, exercise the same care in investigating the situation. Administrative staff members should not become a convenient excuse for alleged misconduct or failure to follow company procedures.

- Develop a corrective action plan that meets the needs of the company, agency or office and agent. Test any corrective action to ensure consistency with prior actions.

- Follow-up to determine that the action plan was implemented on a timely basis and properly resolved the situation.

- If the general agent or agency manager and the agent cannot resolve the situation or issue, the general agent or agency manager should contact the company whose product was sold or whom the agent represented and ask them how to proceed.

- Even if the general agent or agency manager and agent can resolve the problem, the issue, their discussions and the training or developmental action plan should be documented. In this way, the general agent or agency manager can demonstrate that he or she took timely action.

- The general agent or agency manager should investigate whether other instances of potential misconduct or failures to follow company procedures have occurred. For example, if the agent has failed to provide properly completed replacement forms because of a lack of training, might the agent need training on other forms?

- The general agent or agency manager should take precautions to avoid minimizing or overlooking the improprieties of high-performing, successful agents. Ignoring improprieties, making excuses for these agents and providing different levels of action than applied to other agents may give the impression that different standards being applied. This can undermine support for compliance and market conduct in the agency and expose the general agent or agency manager to accusations that he or she failed to supervise properly.

- The general agent or agency manager should increase scrutiny of the agent to ensure that he or she has learned the proper process or procedure and is now following it, thereby avoiding similar compliance issues.

- If the agent has had training responsibility or done joint work with new agents, interview these agents to determine if they have possibly been influenced to use improper behavior.

- Interview the other agents in the office to determine if they have picked up any improper ideas or approaches from the agent.

- If the general agent or agency manager plans to terminate an agent, it is best to act as expeditiously as possible. The agent may learn of the impending termination and act inappropriately with clients, client records or other members of the agency or office.

7

How to Integrate Compliance and Market Conduct into Managing for Success

For a compliance and market conduct system to be effective, it must avoid making compliance a burden on the general agent or agency manager. One way to make a system efficient is to build it into the daily activities that lead to management success. This tactic makes compliance and market conduct just another part of running an agency, instead of something special, additional or tacked on to normal operations of the agency.

Because each general agent or agency manager runs his or her agency differently based on strategy, skills, markets, etc., there is no one way to integrate compliance and market conduct into the daily activities of an agency. The following tips and ideas can help a general agent or agency manager integrate compliance and market conduct into everyday operations. Not every tip will be applicable or appropriate for every general agent or agency manager, and some of the categories used, for example, training and communication, coaching and counseling and supervising productivity, may overlap somewhat because they involve similar activities.

RECRUITING AND SELECTING NEW AGENTS

- Educate sources of referrals about your compliance and market conduct standards and their importance. Help them understand that one of your standards for recruits is high personal ethical standards. Sources of referrals often know aspects of a candidate's character that would cause a manager to question whether the candidate is right for the job. Their sensitivity to your high ethical standards will help them screen out those candidates.

- Set the tone for your agency when you first meet people interested in the business. Explain your compliance and market standards early in the recruiting process. Create the expectation before they become agents that compliance is not something they do after the sale to satisfy someone in the home office—it is the basis for the sale. Emphasize that no matter the agent's level of performance, improper market conduct will lead to disciplinary action.

- Document the steps taken in your selection process, including those that involve screening for compliance and market conduct, and maintain this documentation in your files for use if questions arise. Sometimes this process must be company-specific to include different companies' requirements. Follow the process to ensure you account for every critical step.

- Avoid making compromises in the selection process for a candidate with good marketing potential, but weak ethics. A job candidate who does not deem it necessary to know a product well before selling it may signal a potential problem. Someone who is unconcerned about the suitability of a sale made to a friend may be even less concerned about the suitability of a sale to a stranger.

- Do not rely on the selection screening done by the companies that appoint and offer contracts to candidates. Carefully interview and question candidates to learn about their personal ethics and character.

- Be cautious of candidates who have a large natural market that is either outside the United States or based on foreign nationals. Issues could arise regarding money laundering or language barriers that could lead to potential claims of misrepresentation.

- When candidates are first trying out the job (before they are fully committed) make it clear that sales must be suitable and conducted in a proper way. Ensure that they understand there are no short cuts or easy ways to get around your agency and company standards.

- Demonstrate proper compliance and market conduct standards during joint exploratory sales. Ensure that you (or whomever you delegate joint work to) provide a model sales process that is completely appropriate.

- Make the process of reviewing and signing company ethics statements a significant experience and not just paperwork that must be completed in order to be appointed.

- Explain to a candidate that the company is required to conduct a thorough background check to determine whether the candidate has a criminal record that might prevent insurance company appointment. Emphasize that the candidate should be as truthful and accurate as possible in completing the application.

- Scrutinize all initial, pre-contract sales to ensure they are being conducted properly.

RECRUITING AND SELECTING EXPERIENCED AGENTS

- Do not assume that a problem the agent had with prior business is not your problem. If complaints or problems come up with prior business, they will involve the agent and his or her prior company. However, some general agents or agency managers may fail to appreciate the impact of these problems on their own company or business. In some cases, there is spillover involving a complaint from an agent's tenure with another company to the new company he or she now is associated with.

- Carefully scrutinize currently licensed agents regarding their past performance and standards. Ask them how they would handle situations in which they might have to sacrifice a sale because of ethics. Probe their background for prior complaints and conflicts with clients. Do not be tempted by the potential productivity of an experienced agent who is fleeing his or her past compliance problems.

- Avoid hiring an experienced agent who may want to roll his or her book of business. Caution experienced agents you recruit that replacements of existing policies from their old companies will be examined carefully and that only those that meet agency and company standards will be acceptable.

- Be careful that a big case does not blind you to an experienced agent's potential compliance issues. Some agents will use a big potential case to get a manager to overlook otherwise questionable history.

- Probe the background and compliance history of an experienced agent's associates. If the agent works closely with a CPA or attorney, do not ignore the potential compliance issues related to their work. You also should also probe compensation arrangements between the experienced agent and other professionals he or she works with to determine their appropriateness. If the agent has administrative staff, question them to determine whether the agent has had market conduct problems in the past.

- Carefully examine the markets the experienced agent works in to determine whether they pose risks you should analyze before hiring the agent. For example, if an agent sells predominantly in work-site markets, he or she must exercise care that sales are conducted properly, full disclosure is provided, there are no improper commission or compensation arrangements with individuals in the company, etc. When selecting this agent, the manager would be wise to examine these issues.

- Look carefully at the quality of the experienced agent's book of business. The agent should share with the hiring manager or general agent the type of products sold and the systems used to make those sales. You should be looking for signs of vulnerability, e.g., a high number of replacements, large numbers of sales to seniors, large numbers of annuities in qualified plans, large numbers of small sales with little or no needs analysis, etc.

- Examine whether the experienced agent is licensed in all of the states in which he or she is doing business. Some experienced agents are lax in having an up-to-date license in all states in which they prospect and write business. You also may want to determine whether they have shown a pattern of many changes in license status, suggesting possible problems with meeting continuing education requirements.

- Some experienced agents are unwilling to change their normal administrative procedures to match agency standards. Unless these procedures are in keeping with your agency requirements, a problem could arise. For example, you may have requirements for the contents of client files or for audits and file review. Review your agency's administrative requirements with experienced agents during the selection process to determine whether the agent will be able to adapt to your systems and requirements.

- Observe where the experienced agent came from. If he or she once worked in an environment that accepted improper conduct, will he or she be able to overcome prior experiences? If the agent's prior agency or office was known as being a place where compliance and market conduct was not important, will he or she be able to change perspective in your agency or office? You may want to make inquiries about the agent's prior agency or office to learn more about it.

- Look at who the agent is bringing with him or her. If he or she has support staff or has relationships with other agents or companies, are these people with whom you want to be associated? Interview the experienced agent's administrative staff to gain insight into his or her background and experiences.

- Evaluate the experienced agent's marketing plan. Is it risky? Does he or she plan to sell your products in the correct markets? Is this a market your products are well suited to? Is the plan realistic? Will it place the agent under so much pressure to produce that he or she may be tempted to cut corners?

- Share your agency compliance standards with experienced agents to determine whether they will be able to live by them. For example, some experienced agents may be unwilling to submit their sales materials for approval or may be unwilling to attend mandatory training on new products. A manager must ask whether it is worth hiring an experienced agent who will argue about and resist accepting the agency's compliance standards. The time to determine whether the agent will accept your standards is during the selection process.

- Avoid making special arrangements during the selection process for experienced agents regarding compliance policies or procedures. This can set a bad example for others in the agency. For example, an agent may claim that he or she has a detached office where he or she only sells property and casualty insurance and that you need not supervise that part of the agent's business or audit that office's files. Unless you periodically supervise and audit you will never know whether he or she is conducting life insurance sales from that location. When other agents learn that some agents have a special arrangement, they too will seek exceptions.

- Scrutinize initial or early sales of all new agents to ensure they are being conducted properly.

TRAINING

Agent Training

- Only experienced agents and second line managers who are knowledgeable about compliance and market conduct should be allowed to do joint work with new agents.

- Include a discussion of compliance issues when introducing new products to your agents. Identify potential compliance issues and suggest how agents should be careful to avoid them.

- Ask a representative groups of agents to help review required compliance training so it is relevant and has their support.

- Have agents who are knowledgeable about compliance conduct training sessions to demonstrate that agents are concerned about it.

- If you do not conduct the new agent training on compliance and market conduct, periodically sit in on the sessions to observe that they are being conducted properly.

- Suggest that agents include compliance topics in their sales builder meetings. Help them by providing information they can use or hiring a speaker.

- Require agents to demonstrate product knowledge before being allowed to sell it without close supervision.

- Closely screen any potential training programs suggested by agents, other mangers or vendors. Do not let someone influence your agents with improper sales techniques.

- Obtain a wide range of compliance training materials from the companies you have a relationship with and choose the best to use in your own compliance training.

- Develop agendas that identify the content of your training programs, especially regarding product knowledge and compliance and market conduct. Maintain copies of the agendas so you may document that you provided appropriate training.

- Take attendance at training sessions and maintain a copy of the attendance record in your compliance files. Follow-up on a timely basis with agents who do not attend training. Sometimes compliance and market conduct issues arise from a lack of product knowledge.

- Encourage your agents to attend industry training programs that emphasize professionalism and proper market conduct.

- Make certain that new agents complete all elements of their training as they are brought on board before being allowed to sell on their own.

- Identify the compliance training available in the regular agent training materials you receive from the companies you have a relationship with and make certain that those parts of the training material are used correctly.

- Teach agents the critical administrative steps they must follow for submitting applications and making changes that can help them avoid potential market conduct problems.

- Require all new agents to acknowledge that they have received appropriate compliance and market conduct training. Keep a copy of this acknowledgment—a memo signed by each agent—in your compliance files.

- Require all agents to acknowledge that they have received new product information and training and that they have been alerted to potential compliance and market conduct issues related to the sale of the product. Keep a copy of this acknowledgment—a memo signed by each agent—in your compliance files.

- If you use a specialist to teach courses in advanced markets, such as estate and business planning, ensure that the specialist includes a discussion of the market conduct issues involved in selling in these markets.

- The training material of some companies have been approved for continuing education credit. Attempt to get the most from your training by using accredited training as often as possible. Check with the companies you do business with to find out what they offer.

- Ask experienced agents to identify their compliance and market conduct training needs and use that information to help build training specifically tailored for them.

- Suggest that experienced agents who participate in sales builder programs consider including compliance and market conduct as a discussion topic. Help them find resources, such as speakers or articles, so it is easy for them to do so.

Second Line Manager Training

- Conduct compliance training with all new supervisors or second line managers as part of their regular training.

- Develop agendas for your training programs that identify the content, especially the content on product knowledge, compliance and market conduct. Maintain copies of the agendas so you may document that you provided the appropriate training.

- Teach your second line managers how to spot potential compliance problems early and what to do about them. Use realistic case studies to help them apply this training.

- Require second line managers to become experts in different specific compliance or market conduct areas so they may share their expertise with each other and with agents, e.g., have one become an expert on replacements and another on signature issues.

- Circulate all information on compliance to second line managers and be certain that the material highlights changes in procedures and policies. Follow-up to make certain they understand the changes and can explain them to their agents.

- Require your second line managers to conduct part of the new agent compliance and market conduct training so that they learn it by teaching it.

- Discuss compliance and market conduct issues in your periodic management meetings. Use examples and case studies and ask second line managers how they would handle them.

Administrative Staff Training

- Use real case studies of compliance and market conduct problems to educate administrative staff so they may relate to the importance of compliance and market conduct.

- Have experienced administrative staff help develop compliance and market conduct training materials and job aids used to educate new staff about compliance and market conduct. This will make the training more realistic and relevant.

- Have the agency's administrative staff network with other administrative staff people in other agencies to learn how to avoid administrative issues that could lead to potential market conduct problems.

- Make agent training on compliance available to administrative staff so they understand the requirements agents must follow.

- Stress to administrative staff that responsiveness to client problems, including timely follow-up, is one of the best ways to avoid complaints.

- When a long-term service or highly-effective administrative staff person is leaving, advise the agent to have that person and his or her replacement work together for a period of time to ensure continuity and effective training of the new person. Agents sometimes will object because it involves a higher cost, but the value of a good transition cannot be underestimated.

- Periodically meet with administrative staff to learn their concerns about market conduct and compliance.

■ COMMUNICATION

- Have a compliance bulletin board where changes in compliance policies and procedures are posted to help ensure that everyone finds out about them.

- If you have an agency newsletter, include a compliance section, e.g., "The Compliance Corner," and regularly review important compliance issues.

- If your agency has its own intranet, include an area on it for compliance notices. If possible, include links to the compliance manuals and information from the companies with which you have a relationship.

- Some companies have compliance and market conduct areas on their web sites. Circulate a list of the addresses of these sites or links to them so agents have an easy source of information on compliance and market conduct.

- Make certain that agents and their administrative staff have an easily accessible source of all compliance requirements for each of the companies with which you have a relationship.

- If you have detached offices, make certain that agents in all of the offices receive the same compliance information at the same time. Require them to acknowledge that they have received the information.

- Circulate general information on compliance and market conduct to agents, such as articles from industry newsletters or company magazines.

- Regularly send out information to agents regarding practical advice on handling compliance issues.

- Circulate real cases of proper and improper compliance and market conduct. For example, cases in which an agent finds a way to avoid replacing a client's policy or an agent made a mistake that led to disciplinary action.

- Include compliance topics in routine agency meetings to demonstrate to your agents that compliance and market conduct is ongoing rather than only a response to a problem.

- Include compliance in your annual meeting agenda and make the topics relevant and meaningful.

- If you are going to profile a top agent at an agency meeting or function, carefully check to make certain that the agent has an exemplary market conduct background so you do not inadvertently communicate to the other agents that productivity is more important that market conduct.

- Some agents are unwilling to attend agency meetings. If important compliance and market conduct information is provided at these meetings, they may not be aware of it. Follow-up with a written copy of the information communicated at meetings.

- Be on the watch for agents who pick up sales tools, techniques and ideas from meetings and vendors. These may not be approved sales materials or may involve the agents in potential market conduct problems.

- Hold periodic meetings with agents to find out whether they are being confronted with any compliance or market related issues or roadblocks. Help them develop appropriate solutions to these. For example, agents may be concerned that some sales material is too difficult for clients to understand or that administrative problems may routinely lead to bad feelings on the part of clients.

- Hold periodic meetings with administrative staff to find out whether they are being confronted with compliance or market related issues or roadblocks. Help them develop appropriate solutions to these.

- When sending out information on compliance and market conduct, e.g., new manuals, changes in state regulations, updates on company procedures, etc., keep a list in your compliance files of the recipients of the information.

- Involve your agents in planning for the implementation of compliance initiatives, such as the annual meeting.

- Identify contacts at the companies you do business with who can help agents and their administrative staff answer compliance questions.

- Some companies have programs that support ethics and proper market conduct, such as Ethics Awareness Month. If you have a relationship with these companies, take advantage of their programs to communicate the ongoing importance of ethics and proper market conduct.

- Compliance and market conduct information is as important to an agent as tax information. Some agencies include updates on both topics in the same newsletter or bulletin to reinforce that message.

- If you ask agents who attend conferences, such as MDRT, to make a presentation at an agency meeting about what they learned, suggest that they also discuss any compliance and market conduct topics that were presented.

COACHING AND COUNSELING

- Counsel agents who are in a slump to avoid the temptation to cut corners and force sales.

- Coach agents and sales managers to avoid replacements and instead suggest they focus on new business.

- Coach agents to build their practice based on referrals, because this requires good client relationships, rather than on direct mail, which often leads to weak ones.

- Remind agents to conduct annual reviews even if the likelihood of making a sale is low because ongoing customer contact leads to fewer complaints.

- When problems arise with company questions about applications, explain to agents and their administrative staff that companies have the duty to review the business submitted to them and that this process is not a personal criticism.

- Meet with agents who are having medical problems or who have family members with medical problems to discuss how they plan to continue to do business, because a distraction can lead to possible market conduct issues.

- Counsel agents who are hiring administrative staff to examine their background carefully to avoid individuals who had an ethical problem in a prior job.

- Coach disorganized agents on the potential risks of administrative errors that can lead to compliance and market conduct problems.

- Counsel agents who sell a small number of very large cases each year that they must exercise care that the pressure to close a case does not tempt them to take potential market conduct risks.

- When providing advice on a specific case, such as advice on how to structure a buy/sell case, review with the agent the market conduct issues involved so the agent understands how to avoid any potential problems.

- Maintain notes on coaching and counseling sessions with agents to document that you provided appropriate guidance regarding market conduct and compliance.

- If you have two or more agents that work closely together as a team, be certain that you provide them with the same advice and counsel regarding market conduct and compliance. Do not rely on one agent to share your message with the other.

- Caution agents who do joint work to coordinate their efforts carefully, so potential market conduct issues regarding disclosure of information do not occur. Each agent may tend to assume that the other has provided critical client information.

- In joint-work cases, all the agents involved should be properly licensed in the states in which the client resides or does business. Caution agents that joint-work arrangements should not be used to circumvent licensing requirements.

- Highly productive agents usually are very self-confident and independent. Some of them may be reluctant to follow the details of company policy because they feel their productivity and success demonstrate the superiority of the way they do business. One way to sensitize them to the importance of market conduct and compliance is to educate them about the risks and costs improper conduct can pose for their practice. Exercise care in making exceptions for them and attempt to deal directly with them on compliance and market conduct issues, rather than with their staff or associates.

- Advise agents and their administrative staff to provide adequate room for files if they are relocating offices or redesigning their work areas. Well-designed and ample files can help avoid compliance problems related to documentation and file maintenance.

- Advise agents with high administrative staff turnover to give additional attention to client relations, because high turnover sometimes leads to unsatisfactory responsiveness to clients, which in turn can lead to complaints.

SUPERVISING PRODUCTIVITY

- Meet more frequently with agents who sell in markets that have a greater incidence of compliance issues to review their cases and avoid potential market conduct problems.

- Discuss the reasons for any dramatic decline or increase in business with agents to determine whether it signals a potential market conduct issue.

- Require second line managers to conduct case reviews on a regular basis with all agents during their first year of employment.

- Outline the information you expect you and your second line managers to use regularly to supervise productivity and make certain that it includes compliance and market conduct indicators, so that your supervisory meetings can accomplish all of your goals.

- Meet with new and experienced agents equally often, because years of experience do not guarantee freedom from potential market conduct errors.

- Do not only review applications, but expand your focus to the clients in the agent's target market. Get to know the way your agents market so you may give them pointers on how to avoid potential market conduct problems.

- Question agents who are working intensively in a specific market to determine whether they are cutting corners because they may have developed a standardized process to make sales.

- Discuss how agents with a large geographical territory are handling the difficulty of conducting multiple interviews to be assured that they are not taking any risky shortcuts with signatures, policy delivery and follow-up with clients.

- Suggest to agents with large administrative staffs that they conduct regular performance reviews with them to assure good performance and avoid potential administrative problems that can lead to complaints.

- Ask agents with large administrative staffs how they are keeping in touch with their staff's performance because administrative issues can create complaints.

- If an agent has a performance coach, it often is worthwhile to question the agent periodically on the advice the coach provides. Some coaches do not fully understand compliance and market conduct and may provide advice that is not completely appropriate.

- Exercise caution that you do not ignore reviewing second line manager's personal business as carefully as you review your agents'.

- Agents who work intensively in a specific market sometimes write articles for publications aimed at that market, e.g., a dental association's newsletter. They also may give presentations at meetings. Caution those agents that their presentations and articles must be approved in advance.

- Caution agents who have relationships with several companies that they should attempt to avoid mixing and matching sales materials from different companies in their sales presentations. Clients may become confused about the features and benefits of different products because several different product brochures may have been provided and not well differentiated.

- Agents who do joint work with other professionals, e.g., accountants or attorneys, should be advised that providing fees and sharing commissions must be reviewed carefully to avoid improper compensation arrangements.

- Multi-line agents should be advised to exercise caution that they do not present products as having tie-in relationships unless such a tie-in is sanctioned by a company. For example, some property and casualty insurance companies provide discounts on property and casualty insurance for multiple sales to the same household. To claim a tie-in exists when it does not is an example of misrepresentation.

- Agents with outside business interests should be cautioned to exercise care that they do not link their business dealings inappropriately. For example, an agent who sells real estate should not require that clients of his or her real estate practice purchase property and casualty or life insurance from him or her to obtain a sale.

■ MOTIVATING

- In developing agency sales contests, be careful to temper any competitiveness with cautions regarding proper market conduct and compliance.

- When announcing company contests or sales incentives, emphasize that sales must conform to proper procedures and that they will be scrutinized to ensure that they are proper and avoid potential market conduct issues.

- Prepare for the rush of business in the waning days of an agency or company contest by having enough administrative people and second line managers available to screen the applications and ensure they are proper. Scrutinize this business to make certain that it reflects proper market conduct.

- Brief administrative staff regarding the rules and procedures of contests or incentive programs so they can avoid potential administrative errors that could lead to market conduct problems.

- Caution agents during a contest or incentive program not to pay administrative staff bonuses based on commissions unless they are licensed.

- If top agents from your agency speak at agency meetings, meet with them first to screen what they plan to say so that their comments are in agreement with your market conduct and compliance standards.

- If you or a company disciplines an agent for improper market conduct, increase your contact with the agent to help him or her stay motivated. Sometimes agents who are disciplined become bitter and angry, and this can lead them to make even more market conduct errors.

- As an agent who has been in a slump begins to recover, pay extra attention to his or her business as early as possible in the recovery so any potential market conduct issues can be resolved without derailing that recovery.

- Praise agents who follow proper compliance and market conduct procedures. Although you expect them to do business properly, they deserve acknowledgment and recognition for succeeding in compliance along with everything else.

AGENCY OPERATIONS

Another aspect of integrating compliance into managing for success involves streamlining agency and office procedures. Some compliance problems can be traced to overly complex administrative or compliance procedures. For example, applications are increasingly complicated and require multiple client signatures. An agent may make a mistake on the application and correct it later without getting the proper signature from the client. Or, the number of separate compliance-related forms and brochures required may lead to some being misused, used out of sequence in the sale or simply forgotten. General agents and agency managers should be sensitive to the administrative procedures that can lead to market conduct and compliance problems. Though general agents and agency managers should train and educate the agent and associates to systematize the administrative process and avoid errors, streamlining procedures is an especially valuable way to avoid problems.

Supervising administrative staff is an important part of agency operations. Many general agents and agency managers consider the supervision of administrative staff to be the agent's responsibility. Therefore, ensuring that proper supervision takes place includes teaching agents how to supervise their administrative staff and helping them carry out their responsibility.

The following are some tips agents can use to make monitoring and supervising their administrative staff efficient and effective:

- Have members of the administrative staff work with the agent to simplify procedures that create potential compliance problems for the agent, such as incomplete applications or out-of-date sales materials.

- Have members of the administrative staff attend any meetings or conference calls on compliance and market conduct so they can hear what the agent is being told.

- Encourage administrative staff to share solutions to common administrative, compliance and market conduct issues with each other.

- Ask the administrative staff to create compliance guidelines for their work activities. Have the general agent or agency manager review these guidelines to make certain they are correct.

- Make certain the administrative staff member has a person he or she can contact if compliance and market conduct questions arise.

- The agent should share all compliance information with the administrative staff. Administrative staff should have individual copies of company policy and procedure manuals readily available to them. They should not have to rely on an agency or office copy. The agent should periodically meet with them to review the information and make certain everyone has the same understanding of the procedures and policies. Administrative staff should be involved in any compliance training the agent receives.

- The agent should set an example for his or her administrative staff by paying attention to compliance and market conduct in his or her own work.

- Make certain that administrative staff members who are responsible to support other staff members know the compliance and market conduct implications of their secondary responsibilities.

- Have the agent provide his or her administrative staff with a description of their compliance and market conduct responsibility.

- Have the agent hold regular performance meetings with his or her administrative staff in which compliance and market conduct is discussed. Help the agent develop a checklist of compliance and market conduct related activities to review administrative staff members' activity and performance.

- The general agent and agency manager can offer to review the administrative staff members' procedures to help them avoid making compliance and market conduct errors.

8
Market Conduct and Compliance Examinations and Audits

Market conduct and compliance audits and examinations have become commonplace. The NASDR requires both periodic, unannounced and annual audits of registered representatives whose conduct signals potential market conduct issues. Sometimes these are performed by home office staff; other times companies allow other registered principals in the supervisory chain to conduct them. General agents and agency managers who are registered principals often have to conduct audits of the registered representatives who report to them.

Not all examinations and audits are driven by NASDR requirements. Many general agents and agency managers are required by the companies they have relationships with to conduct periodic examinations to identify potential market conduct issues.

Even if examinations and audits were not required by the NASD or companies, general agents and agency managers would be well advised to use this methodology as part of their overall market conduct and compliance supervisory system.

General agents and agency managers must understand regulator and company market conduct examination procedures as well as how to conduct examinations on their own.

OVERVIEW OF EXAMS AND AUDITS AND THEIR PURPOSE

There are several types of market conduct and compliance examinations and audits:

- regulator (i.e., state and NASDR) examinations of companies;
- company examinations of agents, managers and agencies or offices;
- managerial examinations of agents; and
- agent or manager self-examinations.

The purpose of all of these is to:

- identify potential market conduct and compliance shortcomings or issues;

- identify areas where company procedures may be followed incorrectly;

- provide feedback and direction on how to remove or resolve the issues, errors or deficiencies that were identified and their root cause;

- develop a plan for making any needed changes in procedures, processes or practices; and

- allow the implementation of the plan and ensure that the shortcomings or issues that were identified are appropriately resolved and that future instances are avoided.

An important purpose of market conduct and compliance examinations is to provide an opportunity to assess potential market conduct and compliance risks. Regardless of who does the examination, it can provide insight into where enhancements must be made to policies and procedures to reduce risks. Truly effective examinations look back at what may have been done improperly in the past as well as forward to identify areas where risks may exist in the future.

Examinations or audits are an important responsibility of companies, general agents and agency managers. Though their perspective on some issues may differ, typically they are seeking the same goal, namely, identifying potential areas of non-compliance and taking corrective action to resolve them.

Regulator Exams

Most regulator examinations or audits are of companies and not agencies and offices. Though most regulator examinations of market conduct and compliance are conducted by state regulators, the SEC and NASDR also conduct market conduct and compliance examinations or audits. Audit cycles vary by state, but a triennial audit cycle is typical. Regulators will also audit companies more often if they believe that there are potentially significant market conduct and compliance problems.

State regulators also conduct financial audits of insurance companies on a regular basis. These types of audits will not be discussed.

In general, the following describes elements of all regulator market conduct examinations:

Exams can be on-site, which means that the search for and review of information conducted by the examiners will be conducted at the company's home and field offices. A *desk exam* is a request to review specific company or agency records and is conducted at the regulator's offices.

Exams can be targeted or comprehensive. *Targeted exams* are specific to one or more issues or problems. For example, a regulator may initiate a targeted exam based on received complaints. How the exam is conducted depends on the issue that triggered it.

A *comprehensive exam,* sometimes called a *market conduct audit,* is a review of a wide range of company processes, procedures and operations to determine the propriety of the company's market conduct practices. State regulators may use the NAIC Market Conduct Examiners Handbook to organize and coordinate the examination.*

The NAIC Market Conduct Handbook identifies the areas where a company must evaluate its market conduct practices and outlines processes and procedures for determining whether its market conduct is adequate. Sometimes the comprehensive market conduct exam is part of a regulator's overall financial examination or audit, rather than a separate exam. However, because of regulator concerns about market conduct, the frequency of independent or stand-alone comprehensive market conduct examinations has increased.

Many regulators tailor their market conduct audits based on their experience with various types of companies. Most regulators' examiners have great latitude in their audit procedures.

A multi-state exam is used when two or more state regulators coordinate their investigations. States agree on how to conduct the exam, then hire staff depending on how they plan to cooperate. Multi-state examinations are conducted most often when several states are concerned about a company's market conduct, and that company has large blocks of similar business in several states.

The NAIC Examination Tracking System (ETS) is a computer database state regulators use to coordinate the scheduling of examinations. The NAIC ETS helps prevent state regulators from scheduling conflicting examinations and helps them coordinate multi-state examinations. It also helps state regulators share the results of their audits and examinations.

Typically, agents and field management do not directly get involved in targeted or comprehensive regulator market conduct examinations or audits. In some cases, agency managers or general agents may be asked to provide information to a company that results in the company auditing an agent's practice or an agency or office's operation. State regulators have also been known to visit a random sample of agents or offices to conduct an independent audit of the agent's practices or the agencies' or offices' operation. Audits of agents, agencies and offices may occur when the regulator's examination uncovers potential market conduct improprieties that require further investigation. Sometimes, regulator examinations identify agents who may have committed market conduct errors or improper supervisory practices.

Regulator examinations or audits can be very time consuming for home office staff. The exams require the company to provide records, documentation of procedures,

---

* For additional information about the handbook and its specific contents, visit the NAIC web site at http://www.naic.org.

etc., for the examiners' review. Market conduct audits often can take months to complete.

Companies normally do not receive much advance notice of examinations. Regulators typically contact companies before a comprehensive exam, but the advance notice can vary from 30 to 60 days. For targeted exams (either on site or desk) there may be no notice other than the requirement to provide information within a set period of time.

How the examination is conducted or organized depends on many factors:

- Have problems in the past required follow-up?

- Are there patterns of complaints against the company?

- Do general, industry-wide issues require investigation, such as internal replacements?

- Do factors such as mergers and acquisitions require examination?

- Which new regulations have taken effect since the last examination, and can the company provide evidence that it complied with the new regulations?

For a comprehensive examination, the examiners normally use a sampling procedure to check the processing of important transactions, like claim handling and complaints. Regulators will review carefully all complaint, replacement and form filing logs, administrative procedures such as licensing and appointments, etc., to determine whether they meet state standards.

Regulators usually look both at the existence of proper standards, processes and procedures as well as evidence that the company uses the processes and procedures on a consistent basis. For example, in states that require the company to have an anti-fraud plan, examiners will review the plan and determine whether the company is carrying it out. They will determine whether the company has communicated the plan to the proper home office and field personnel and ensure that it monitors potentially fraudulent activities according to the plan.

Targeted exams, whether on site or desk, focus on one or a small number of specific issues, and the information reviewed pertains to them. For example, assume the state has received a number of complaints from senior citizens regarding a company's improper marketing tactics. Although these complaints may have been logged over a 12-month period and resolved individually, the pattern may prompt the state to investigate the company to determine whether there are additional cases that have not yet resulted in a complaint to the state. A regulator may ask to review a sample of all the company's sales made to senior citizens during the appropriate time period and review each case to look for evidence of improper practices. The regulator may interview clients, agents and home office personnel as part of the audit.

Targeted examinations also can be triggered by the results of comprehensive examinations. For example, in an examination of one multi-line company a state may identify that it has consistently failed to provide full disclosure regarding tie-in sales between life insurance and property and casualty. This may cause the state to conduct a targeted examination of other multi-line companies to determine whether the same problems exist.

Over the last several years, the NASDR has conducted sweeps of a large number of companies on specific issues, such as suitability of annuity sales. These are targeted audits of a specific issue. The NASDR typically will require very specific information from a company regarding the implementation and operation of procedures its rules and regulations require.

Once the examination (comprehensive or targeted) has been completed, a preliminary report often is provided to the company to alert them to problems that were identified. At this time, the company can respond to the preliminary findings with additional information for clarification purposes. A final report then is issued that includes all of the problems identified by the examination and how the regulator recommends they be resolved. The company can respond to these recommendations and work with the regulator to develop a plan that both the company and regulator find satisfactory. In some cases, the company may decide to request a formal hearing on the report because of differences of opinion regarding the findings. If the examination is a state regulator audit, its findings are entered into the NAIC ETS once it is finalized. The regulator then orders the necessary changes.

If the company is found in violation of state regulations, it may be fined. If the violations are serious enough, the company could lose its license to sell in that state. Fines vary depending on the number of individual violations and their severity. The NASDR also will levy fines and sanctions against broker-dealers, representatives and members of management if it finds violations.

Company Market Conduct Examinations

Companies always have reviewed or audited their own operations, but now they are conducting market conduct examinations of agents and offices more often because of increased industry attention to the subject. Not only are more agents and offices being examined, but the frequency of examinations also is increasing. Some companies that were conducting agent or office examinations every several years are now conducting them annually.

Some companies have begun to include market conduct in the regular financial audits of their agents and offices or to conduct audits specifically to evaluate market conduct and compliance. Often, companies will conduct targeted exams or audits in response to complaints or other indicators that improper market conduct practices may be taking place.

Many general agent and agency manager contracts include language about the company's right to review agency, office agent and manager's books and records to conduct audits and examinations. Some companies have added the explicit right to conduct examinations to their contracts.

Company examinations range from simple requests for information to on site examinations involving the review and analysis of client files, administrative records and procedures, computer files, etc. Sometimes a company will base the examination or audit on a large geographical area, such as a territory, region or zone, or all of the agents or offices in a state. In many cases, rather than examine every agent, the company will draw a sample from all of the agents and survey them with a detailed questionnaire. It may follow-up and actually visit some of the agents, but in many cases a survey is sufficient.

The company examination may be conducted by local management, the company's auditing or compliance functions or an outside auditing or consulting firm. Typically, advance planning for the examination will include a review of company records, particularly the results of prior examinations (action plans, current production and activity, complaint history, replacement history, etc.)

Company market conduct and compliance examiners typically are qualified by training and experience to conduct examinations. They usually are knowledgeable about marketing and sales processes and practices, sales materials and client relations. The examination may be conducted by a single examiner or a team, depending on the size of the agency or office and the extent of the examination.

The NASDR requires broker-dealers to conduct unannounced audits. For NASDR purposes, an unannounced on site audit is required for all offices, including ones with only one or two independent agents who are registered representatives of a broker-dealer. Enforcement actions by the SEC have demonstrated that failure to conduct such audits is seen as a serious failure to provide adequate supervision.* In some cases, these unannounced audits are conducted by local management, if they are registered principals, or by the broker-dealer's home office staff. The issues that typically are reviewed during an NASDR audit are listed in a later section.

If the agency or office is not examined on an annual basis, it often is chosen either at random or based on specific factors that suggest an examination would be of value. Some of these factors are:

- Have problems in the agency or office in the past required follow-up (e.g., has the agency or office carried out all aspects of the last examination's action plan)?

- Are there patterns of complaints involving the agency or office?

- Has the company received information via company sources (e.g., a company hotline, that problems may exist in the agency or office)?

- Have company monitoring procedures identified potential improper conduct, e.g., a higher than average level of replacements?

- Do the markets in which the agents sell pose any greater than normal market conduct or compliance risks (e.g., sales to seniors and work-site marketing)?

- Has agency or office turnover been high or were a number of experienced agents hired who may not have experience with the company's compliance and market conduct procedures?

---

* See, for example, SEC Docket 1606 (Jan. 1997), *In the Matter of Royal Alliance Associates, Inc.,* 63.

- Have company-wide issues required examination, e.g., feedback from home office sources that consumers, in general, may not be receiving sales materials about the features of a product?

- Are new company policies and procedures being used appropriately, e.g., new file documentation requirements?

- Have regulators been concerned about the sale of specific products or sales to specific markets that warrant additional scrutiny, e.g., sales to seniors?

- Which new regulations have taken effect since the last examination, and is the agent or office in compliance with them?

- Is the administrative or management staff in the agency or office new or inexperienced?

- Has the agency or office merged with another since the last examination?

Another important factor that dictates the scope of a company examination is the number of serious improprieties or deficiencies the company identifies as it conducts the examination. If it finds a large number of deficiencies during an examination, the company may expand its scope. For example, if a company samples agent files for review and finds several undelivered policies in an agent's files, this would prompt them to expand their review to all agents' files for all policies sold since the last examination.

In some cases, a company reviews data, such as persistency, replacements, complaints, markets, etc., before conducting an examination to identify agents whose practice may warrant additional scrutiny because of the risk of market conduct or compliance issues. Although typically the general agent, agency manager or agent is not told why he or she was selected for the additional scrutiny, this may explain why companies target specific practices or agents when they examine or audit an agency or office.

HOW A GENERAL AGENT OR AGENCY MANAGER CAN MAKE COMPANY MARKET CONDUCT EXAMINATIONS EFFECTIVE

A company market conduct examination can be a valuable experience, although to some agents, general agents, agency managers and administrative staff it may seem unproductive and intrusive. An examination by a well-trained and knowledgeable compliance professional can help identify potential problems before they create significant risks for agents, general agents, agency managers and companies.

Though a general agent or agency manager cannot make a company examination totally painless, he or she can minimize its disruption of the agency or office.

An examiner is not an adversary. He or she is an unbiased set of ears and eyes who can help the agent, general agent and agency manager uncover problems before they become crises. Just as a smoke detector provides a warning before serious damage is done by a fire, an examiner provides a warning before serious compliance problems occur. Market conduct examinations can identify training needs and areas where procedures must be strengthened. In the long run, an examination, like a medical check up, can lead to advice on how to stop bad habits and stay healthy.

The information presented in this section of the guide applies equally well to the examination performed by companies and broker-dealers.

One of the biggest challenges to a general agent or agency manager who has relationships with several companies is that more than one of them may want to examine his or her agency or office during the year. Though companies typically conduct examinations only of agencies and offices with which they have a significant relationship, several companies still could conduct examinations during a given time period.

The key to making an examination as painless and valuable as possible is to prepare, communicate and cooperate.

HOW A GENERAL AGENT OR AGENCY MANAGER CAN PREPARE FOR AN EXAMINATION OR AUDIT

Everyone in the office should know what to expect when the examination takes place. They should know far in advance what standards the company will use to evaluate their operations and conduct. They should have the opportunity to review their own operations in advance to identify where they need improvement. This should be based on a careful self-assessment of their operation. Information on how to conduct a self-assessment is included in another section of this guide. If a company pre-audit questionnaire exists, it should be completed accurately and fully and sent back to the examiner by the requested date.

In some cases, the general agent or agency manager may be notified of an examination anywhere from a few days to several weeks in advance. He or she may get a telephone call or written notice that explains the process that will be used to conduct the examination and confirms the intended date of the visit. However, some examinations are required to be unannounced, e.g., certain NASDR examinations. A general agent or agency manager should know the frequency of any company examinations. If he or she is uncertain how often a company will examine the agency or office, he or she should ask the company for clarification.

Once a general agent or agency manager is notified that an examination is planned, it is natural to want to clean things up a bit before the examiners arrive. One of the key purposes of an examination is to provide feedback, so cleaning things up can be self-defeating and may hinder the effective evaluation of the general agent or agency manager's processes and procedures.

Any destruction, concealment or falsification of information or documents will turn a minor problem into a major one. It is far better to have any noncompliance or market conduct problems discovered during the normal course of an examination or audit than during an investigation of an alleged cover-up.

The best approach to take when notified of an examination is to let the examiners see how things really are operating and get their feedback. If problems exist, an enhancement plan will be developed and the agent, general agent or agency manager will be given an opportunity to improve and re-align policies, procedures and practices.

Tips on Preparing for an Examination

- Ask the company in advance what the standards are for the examination. Review the standards and identify potential areas where agents and administrative staff may have questions. Get answers to those questions in advance.

- If you know that problems exist in the agency or office, share them with the examiner in advance and ask to develop a plan for dealing with them during the examination.

- Review prior examination reports to identify potential areas where there may be questions.

- Ask other general agents or agency managers who have been examined by this company for impressions of the examinations and suggestions for how to for prepare for one.

- Find out what the examiners will need to carry out the examination (e.g., a locked office, telephone, copier access, etc.) and prepare it for them.

- If the examination is planned for an inappropriate or inconvenient date, ask the company to consider rescheduling. For example, if the general agent and two other agents will be at a company conference during the time scheduled for the examination, it would wise to reschedule.

- If other companies have conducted examinations and their results were positive, share those results with the examiners. If their results were negative, determine whether those results are germane to the other company's examination. If they are, be prepared to share them.

COMMUNICATION ISSUES INVOLVED IN AN EXAMINATION

When the examination begins, those conducting it should be clear in their expectations for the examination, particularly what they hope to learn and how they will provide feedback. Agents, managers and administrative staff should be open and honest about their procedures and how they conduct their business. Everyone should avoid the natural tendency to challenge the reason for the examination and instead focus on making the examination as valuable as possible.

The examiners should keep the general agent or agency manager informed of their progress throughout the examination and share their findings before they leave. They should present their initial findings in an unbiased way and focus on suggested enhancements. The final report should be clear, understandable and focus on the strengths as well as the potential weaknesses found in the office's operations and procedures. The report should be timely and confidential.

At the end of the examination, the manager or agent should meet with the examiner to discuss the general results. Sometimes it is difficult to listen to feedback about potential compliance issues or gaps without becoming defensive. The purpose of the feedback is to develop an enhancement plan. The examination cannot achieve its objectives unless the feedback is specific and direct, so the examiners must be candid. The managers and agents who listen to learn get more value from the examination than those who excuse and rationalize potential shortcomings.

Tips on Communication Issues Related to an Examination

- If the date if the examination is known in advance, let people in the agency or office know of the details of the examination far in advance.

- Set up regularly scheduled meetings with the examiners before they begin. Once they begin, you should both adhere to the schedule.

- Obtain a firm date when feedback will be provided.

- Limit the number of people involved in the initial feedback session so the results can be kept as confidential as possible.

- Have the examiners review their results with the general agent or agency manager in terms of the frequency and severity of each deficiency or error.

- As soon as it is feasible, meet with the entire agency or office and provide them with an overview of the examination process. Set correct expectations of the examination's impact.

- Clarify or any questions with the examiners before they leave the agency or office. Be certain that their feedback is clear.

- Document the feedback the examiners provide for the agency or office files.

- If the general agent or agency manager believes the results of the examination are inaccurate, ask the examiners to conduct additional testing to confirm their initial findings.

HOW AN AGENCY OR OFFICE CAN COOPERATE WITH EXAMINERS

A surprise examination cannot be planned for, but once it is announced, everyone should do everything possible to make key people available. Before the audit begins, the manager or agent should explain to the people in the office why an examination is being conducted, how it will be conducted and who will be involved. The manager or agent should wholly endorse and voice his or her support of it. The examiners' requests for information, space, access to files, etc., should be fulfilled as far as possible.

During the examination, everyone should provide the resources and information the examiner needs. The manager, agent or lead service staff member should meet with the examiners periodically during the examination to ensure they are receiving cooperation from employees. If they are not, the manager should take action to correct this problem.

Examiners often have questions about what they have seen or heard. Explanations provided by agents, administrative staff and managers are invaluable for gaining a full understanding of the situation. All of them, therefore, should be available to answer the examiner's questions.

Tips on Maximizing Cooperation

- Introduce the examiners to the agency or office personnel, describe the importance of their role and voice your support.

- Ensure that examiners have the space and facilities they need to conduct the examination.

- Alert agents and administrative staff in advance that the examiners will need access to files, computers, offices, etc., so that examiners do not have problems with access.

- Inform agents and administrative staff that the examiners will be asking them questions about what they know and the procedures they follow and that their answers will be part of the examination's findings. Suggest that they carefully consider their answers before giving them.

- When explaining the purpose of the examination, emphasize the potential benefits to the agents of knowing whether issues exist before they become serious problems.

- Make it clear to agents that cooperation with the examiners is required and that a lack of cooperation is unacceptable.

- Keep agency or office staff informed of the examination's progress.

- Repeatedly voice your support for the examination during and after the process.

- Stay in touch with agents and administrative staff during the audit and quickly resolve any problems.

HOW COMPANIES CONDUCT EXAMINATIONS

Company examinations typically are based on file reviews, interviews with agents and administrative staff and observation.

File reviews can be in-depth or specific. In-depth reviews usually are extensive case reviews where all market conduct and compliance aspects of a sale are examined. For example, some companies will review a random sample of client files to evaluate suitability, identify hidden replacements, ensure the presence of proper documentation, etc. A case review requires the company to analyze the sale based on the contents of the client file and company records and to determine if it was conducted properly. A case review should be done only by examiners with the training and experience to be able to evaluate sales, marketing materials, illustrations, procedures, etc. A checklist that can be used to screen cases appears later in this guide.

Most companies can review only a sample of sales on an in-depth basis because of the time and number of examiners involved. Sometimes companies will target specific agents based on information regarding their sales practices, markets or specific types of sales, e.g., clients with several annuity purchases in a one-year period.

Some companies will conduct a file review for a specific purpose. For example, during one cycle of examinations, a company reviewed a sample of cases sold during the prior 12 months to determine whether delivery receipts were present in the file. This was done because the company had implemented a requirement that a signed delivery receipt be maintained in the client file during the prior year.

Specific file reviews require less time, less-skilled examiners and often will involve a larger sample of files.

Some companies also will include a survey of clients in their market conduct and compliance examinations. For example, a company may survey a random sample of policyholders via telephone or mail to determine whether hidden replacements exist. This will be done before the agency or office examination and will indicate the agents and files that merit the closest scrutiny.

Examiners will interview agents and administrative staff to determine their level of knowledge about market conduct and compliance policies and procedures, to provide clarification on what the examiner has observed or found and to determine whether the agent or administrative staff has observed any potentially improper activities in the agency or office.

Frequently examiners also will observe the agency and office to identify any market conduct issues. Observation can range from reviewing computer files to checking the agency or office supplies to determining whether out-of-date sales materials are being stocked.

WHAT EXAMINERS LOOK FOR

Appendix F, "Listing of Potential Examination Points," provides a list of questions an examiner might ask when examining an agency or office. This list is meant to provide an example only. Companies tailor their examination points to fit the needs, timing and resources available for an examination.

For each examination point, a trained examiner would gather information perform an evaluation and then document both. Depending on the examination point, the examiner might review all information or survey information. For example, when reviewing the agency or office's compliance communication file to determine whether it contains all company compliance and market conduct communications, the examiner might review all of the company communications since the last examination was conducted or review the file to make certain that specific communications were filed. Interviews should be recorded and the results documented. Some companies use a standardized questionnaire as the basis for collecting interview data.

In most cases, the examiner has standards for evaluating the examination point. For example, the examiner may compare the contents of the agency or office communications file with a home office list of communications. For agent files, the company may have set requirements for client files in its policy and procedures manuals or guides. The file requirements are provided to the examiner as supporting material to assist the evaluation.

Based on the results of his or her review, the examiner might identify one or more potential deficiencies in policy, procedure, implementation or execution.

In some cases, the evaluation of the examination point is open to interpretation. For example, a review of a case file and the subsequent interview with the agent may convince the examiner that the agent failed to disclose the potential negative impact of a replacement adequately. Examiners have to be well trained and experienced to make these judgments.

Documenting the data collected often is a time consuming task. Examiners should be able to identify the specific information collected or reviewed and the results of their reviews from their notes. Failure to adequately document the process can leave the examiner open to criticism if specific evidence is lacking to support accusations that problems or procedural errors exist.

HOW COMPANIES SHARE EXAMINATION RESULTS WITH THE GENERAL AGENT OR AGENCY MANAGER

Some company examinations use an incidence or summary sheet that lists each potential deficiency or discrepancy between company standards and the agency or office policy or procedures. This summary sheet becomes the basis for the feedback the examiner provides to the general agent or agency manager.

Some companies have a policy of not sharing the actual data the examiners collect with the general agent or agency manager, e.g., the specific files reviewed and the potential errors found. They will provide only summaries. If the general agent feels that such information would be valuable, he or she should contact the company's compliance or auditing department because the examiner normally does not have the authority to deviate from the examination process.

The general agent or agency manager should question the examiner regarding the procedures used in the examination. If possible, the general agent or agency manager should get examples of the procedures used to conduct the examination. This will clarify how the process was conducted and how to interpret the results of the examination.

General agents and agency managers should request a written summary of the examination results rather than just verbal feedback from the examiners. A discussion between the general agent or agency manager and the examiners about the results of the examination can be valuable, but it does not replace a written report.

If the examiner is unprepared to provide a written summary following the examination, the general agent or agency manager should have someone present during the discussion to take notes and serve as a witness. A general agent or agency manager should listen carefully to the examiner's feedback. It sometimes is better to ask detailed questions when the examination is fresh in the examiner's mind.

Often the examiner will provide only a high level overview of the results of the examination upon completion. He or she often wants to return to the home office to review notes and develop recommendations. This can be frustrating to some general agents and agency managers because of the uncertainty of the examination results. Companies have a responsibility to provide feedback on their examinations in a timely fashion. A company that takes months to provide feedback is not helping the general agent or agency manager use the examination effectively to prevent problems.

Some companies will provide a written report to the general agent or agency manager following the examination. Often this report will identify the potential market conduct deficiencies and the plan for resolving them. General agents and agency managers should review this report carefully to determine whether it accurately reflects their understanding of policies and procedures in the agency or office. Sometimes issues taken out of context become overblown. For example, there may have been out-of-date illustration software found on agents' computers. Although this sounds significant, there may have been three out-of-date versions of software on only one agent's old computer, which was not even linked to the agency or office's server. Sometimes the general agent or agency manager can help put the examination findings into perspective.

Once there is agreement on the findings, any developmental action plans (i.e., the steps needed to resolve potential compliance issues) should be reviewed carefully and tailored to the agency or office's circumstances. Sometimes developmental action plans are not as specific to an agency or office as they could be because they are developed at the home office following the investigation without the direct input of the general agent or agency manager. Many companies provide the general agent or agency manager with an opportunity to review the proposed plan and comment on it before putting it in place.

If deficiencies are found, the developmental plans should clearly describe the actions required to resolve them, who is responsible for taking action, the standards that will be used to determine whether action has been taken properly, the time frame for completion and the date of any follow-up.

■ NASD REQUIREMENTS FOR AUDITS AND EXAMINATIONS

NASDR Conduct Rule 3010 (also see NASDR Notice to Members 99-45) states that each NASD member firm must establish a supervisory system that, at a minimum, carries out regular internal inspections of both branch offices and registered representatives.

Branch Office Examinations

The objective of branch office examinations is to inspect and examine branch office adherence to procedures and NASDR regulations annually. The examination also verifies that supervisory procedures are being followed and that appropriate oversight of registered representatives and their business is taking place. Typically, the examination is conducted by a designated home office principal, though, depending on the organizational structure of the broker-dealer, this could be a registered principal at a regional or zone level.

Most broker-dealers use a combination of file review and observation when conducting the branch office examination. Often a form will be completed and signed by the branch office registered principal and the home office examiner. All branch office examinations should be documented, signed and dated by the examiner. Examination reports should be maintained indefinitely in case questions arise about the quality of the broker-dealer's supervision.

REGISTERED REPRESENTATIVE EXAMINATIONS

NASDR Conduct Rule 3010 also outlines supervisory responsibilities, including the expectation that on site inspections or examination will be conducted. The purpose of an on site representative examination is to monitor the representative's securities and nonsecurities related activities and to detect and prevent potential regulatory and compliance issues. The feedback from this type of examination can help a representative avoid problems.

Typically these examinations focus on verifying that the representative's sales materials are current, required documents (manuals, reports, files) are maintained, adequate and appropriate fact-finding is done to determine suitability of product recommendations and customer files contain appropriate and adequate documentation.

All registered representatives should be examined annually. If the representative is a member of another representative's administrative staff, his or her examination typically is combined with the examination of the representative with whom he or she works. If the representative is a member of the management staff of the branch office, his or her examination often is combined with the branch office examination.

The examination may be conducted by the registered principal with supervisory responsibility for the representative or a registered principal from the home office.

All representative examinations should be documented, signed and dated by the examiner. All documentation should be maintained indefinitely in case questions arise regarding the quality of the registered principal's supervision.

Often a form or questionnaire is used to guide and document the examination. A sample of a registered representative examination record form is provided in Appendix G. This questionnaire would be used by a registered principal as a guide to conducting an on site examination. The questionnaire presented is not meant to serve as a model and is provided for illustrative purposes only. Broker-dealers tailor their questionnaires to fit their representatives' markets, their products and their supervisory structure.

In those cases where problems may exist (such as the receipt of a significant number of complaints, prior disciplinary records or excessive replacements), an unannounced visit may be appropriate. The NASDR has stressed that unannounced visits or examinations may be appropriate in cases where improprieties or misconduct may exist. Some broker-dealers allow registered principals with supervisory responsibility to conduct unannounced examinations of their own accord, while others require that the broker-dealer's compliance department be notified first.

If there is a suspicion that records or files will be altered or destroyed if advance notice of an examination is given, then an unannounced examination clearly is warranted. Not all unannounced visits, however, are motivated by indications of potential improprieties. Some broker-dealers routinely conduct unannounced examinations of representatives and branch offices.

Some companies and broker-dealers require agents or registered representatives to complete a questionnaire that deals with key company and NASDR regulations annually. Section 4 (Interview) of the questionnaire presented in Appendix G lists the type of questions that often are asked.

These questionnaires can serve as an annual reminder of key company and broker-dealer standards. For example, some questionnaires ask the registered representative to self-report whether or not they have violated any NASDR regulations, such as the using unapproved sales material. Completing this questionnaire may take place as part of the broker-dealer's annual meeting or as part of an annual examination.

Registered principals should review the questionnaires for the registered representatives they supervise, to identify whether potential violations of broker-dealer procedures require further investigation. This review serves as good documentation that the broker-dealer actively sought out information. Evidence that a registered representative provided false information on the self-report questionnaire tends to support the assertion that the registered representative was conscious of improprieties and actively tried to hide them.

Some companies also require agents who are not registered representatives to complete a similar questionnaire on an annual basis. The general agent or agency manager should review those questionnaires for potential violations of company procedures that require further investigation.

HOW TO PERIODICALLY EXAMINE AGENT AND AGENCY OR OFFICE COMPLIANCE AND MARKET CONDUCT

It is in the best interest of the general agent or agency manager to periodically examine the compliance and market conduct practices or his or her agents and agency or office. Periodic examinations provide agents and administrative staff with motivation to maintain standards. Failure to periodically examine agent and administrative conduct creates the impression that standards are unimportant. In addition, periodic review by the general agent or agency manager can identify problems before company or broker-dealer examinations are conducted.

Regular supervision as outlined in earlier sections of this guide provides the general agent or agency manager with ongoing information about potential compliance and market conduct issues. This is valuable information, but it does not reduce the need for periodic examinations of agent files, computers, offices, etc. Periodic examinations are valuable for identifying a wide range of issues, such as use of improper or unapproved sales material, improper file maintenance, failure to follow company procedures, etc., that might not be identified through regular supervision.

Before examining agent market conduct, it is prudent to develop an overall examination strategy that should take into account the size of agency or office, the markets agents are working in, the experience of the agents, the potential compliance risks of their marketing procedures, the locations the agents work in and the other factors, including the requirements set by the companies with which the general agent or agency manager has relationships. Some companies require annual examinations; others require biennial. General agents and agency managers who have relationships with companies that do not require examinations have a more difficult task because they do not have company-required procedures to use as a starting point.

It is best to combine as many companies' requirements into the examination process as possible. A good place to begin is by collecting all of the company requirements and tools (guides, questionnaires, etc.) so that a single examination process can be used to satisfy both general agent or agency manager examination objectives and any company objectives. Examinations take time and energy and should be done as efficiently as possible. Combining requirements can reduce the intrusiveness of examinations on agents and administrative staff by reducing the number of times questions are asked, files are reviewed, etc.

Appendixes F and G provide examples of the types of information that can be reviewed as part of an agent, agency or office examination.

Earlier sections of this chapter discuss how to communicate about, prepare for and gain cooperation for company examinations. The ideas in these sections also should be applied to general agent and agency manager examinations.

General agents and agency managers often use a company's required examination process as a basis for their own examinations. They add issues to the examination process issues that they believe help them reduce compliance and market conduct risk. For example, some general agents and agency managers closely review an agent's web site, e-mail communications, etc., to identify possible compliance issues; others make a point of reviewing each location in which the agent has an office.

If the general agent or agency manager is the agent's registered principal, he or she will be required to follow an examination process outlined by the broker-dealer. Some general agents and agency managers combine the annual registered representative examination with their own examination. Though the registered representative's examination covers a wide range of issues, it typically focuses on only a subset of all issues that should be examined. Therefore, the general agent or agency manager should not rely on it as the only agent examination. For example, issues related to suitability and replacements of traditional products are not covered in a registered representative examination.

General agent and agency manager examinations should be as well documented, as rigorous and objective and no less formal than a company examination. There is a tendency among some general agents and agency managers to be less formal with their own examinations than those required by the companies with which they have a relationship. For example, some general agents and agency managers conduct mini examinations quarterly or semi-annually. They may review a small number of files at one examination, computer contents at another and office content at a third. Though this strategy can be effective, unless the general agent or agency manager carefully documents his or her findings and carefully organizes the examination process, he or she may not be consistent and detailed enough to gain real benefits from these mini-examinations.

A general agent or agency manager should document his or her examination process. Some general agents and agency managers develop an examination checklist to help organize the process and develop a set of tools for conducting the examination and documenting the results. The questionnaire provided in Appendix G is an example of one way to document and organize the examination process; another, somewhat less structured example is presented in Appendix H. It demonstrates how a general agent or agency manager can incorporate several company requirements in the same questionnaire.

HOW TO REVIEW CASE FILES

Case or file review is an important part of the agent examination process. For general agents and agency managers who do not have an examination procedure for case file review, the checklist in Appendix H, "A Sample Case or File Review Checklist," can serve as a basis for developing one tailored to their agents.

When reviewing case files, it sometimes is best to select a random sample of cases that reflect sales that have occurred since the last examination. The size of the sample should be large enough to provide a basis for evaluating the agent's market conduct, but not so large that it creates a barrier to completing the examination.

The number of files selected typically depends on the agent's markets, the products sold and the number of sales. There is no easy way to estimate the number of cases to review. If an agent has made 50 sales since the last examination, of which 40 (80%) were registered products, the sample selected should reflect this 80/20 split. A total sample of 10 cases that reflect the 80/20 product split should be a sufficient sample. If the agent made fewer than 50 sales, the number of cases reviewed most likely should be approximately 10. For agents who sell more than 50 cases, the number of files reviewed should be increased, but generally no more than 20. These are rough guidelines that should be applied with common sense.

The general agent or agency manager should take notes on each file identifying potential issues as well as acceptable compliance with company, agency and office policies and procedures.

If the general agent or agency manager delegates responsibility for file review, he or she should make certain that whoever does the review is qualified and has the training and tools necessary to carry out the responsibility properly.

HOW TO REVIEW COMPUTER FILES

The goal of reviewing computer files typically is to identify unapproved software, potentially improper sales materials, potentially improper market conduct, out-of-date software and, for registered representatives, unapproved correspondence.

All computers (desktop and laptop) in all locations as well as the content of backup media (tapes, disks, CDs, etc.) should be examined. This should include the computers of administrative staff. If the computers are networked, all individual computers should be examined, as well as the server's centralized files.

Some general agents and agency managers organize their examinations into three parts:

- required programs that must be up-to-date (e.g., illustration programs);
- unapproved software; and
- unapproved correspondence.

The examination should begin with the directory of all programs and files. Titles of programs can provide insight into their content. General agents and agency managers should have a list of all approved computer programs. These programs should be present, properly installed and up-to-date. If the date of the version of programs cannot be determined, the programs' backup material may provide information.

Many computers have software that allows for searches, such as Windows Explorer. The general agent or agency manager can use these programs to identify programs and files that might identify unauthorized software. The following searches can help identify improper or unapproved software or correspondence:

- key words, e.g., financial, planning, estate, illustration, analysis, investment, etc.;
- key abbreviations, e.g. (fin, plng, ff, etc.);
- all directories, subdirectories and files; and
- client names, especially recent clients.

If these searches do not identify e-mail correspondence, a subsequent search should be conducted of the web portals the agent uses for e-mail to determine whether electronic correspondence is proper. Often old e-mail correspondence is stored in a subdirectory or an archive on the PC. Review of e-mail correspondence is especially important for registered representatives because many broker-dealers have procedures that should be followed for reviewing their e-mail correspondence.

Any suspicious programs should be run to determine their purpose. For example, a program called *Financial Projector* should be accessed and run to see what it provides.

If the search must be limited, restrict it to the time frame since the last examination.

Each computer should be set for the correct date and file dates should correspond appropriately.

The general agent or agency manager should take notes on the results of the examination. In some cases, copies of printouts or correspondence should be made to provide examples to support the examination's conclusions.

REVIEWING WEB SITES

The goal of reviewing agent, agency or office web sites typically is to identify unapproved content, potentially improper sales materials, improperly licensed activities and, for registered representatives, unapproved correspondence.

General agents or agency managers without the computer knowledge and experience needed to carry out this evaluation should find someone in the agency, at a company they have a strong relationship with or a local expert or consultant to help.

The entire content of all web sties should be reviewed as well as related e-mail correspondence, downloads, backups, etc. Any prior versions of the site also should be reviewed, as should links between sites.

Some general agents and agency managers organize their examinations into four parts:

- determining that the site's content has been approved by the registered representative's broker-dealer and the companies with which the agent has a relationship;

- determining that the agent has not engaged in the sale of insurance products and services in jurisdictions for which he or she does not hold a valid license;

- unapproved correspondence through the site; and

- inappropriate links to and from other sites.

The content of web sites is treated the same way any other sales material is. It should be reviewed and approved before use, agents should provide documentation that this has been done, and the site should match the version that was approved. Any modifications made to the site also should be reviewed and approved.

The general agent or agency manager should attempt to get a paper or electronic copy of the site's contents as documentation. A listing of all contact with the site and replies to those contacts should be obtained. If there are large numbers of contacts, then a sampling approach should be used. If the agent provides quotes via the site, samples of those messages should be obtained and reviewed. If the site has a calculator or some other functionality, it should be tested. For example, if the site provides an analysis of retirement need based on age, gender, marital status, current financial circumstances, etc., the accuracy and appropriateness of the calculations should be tested for a range of possible clients.

The general agent or agency manager should take notes on the results of the review and clearly identify which screen or page of the site is being referred to. In some cases, copies of printouts or correspondence should be made to provide examples to support the examination's conclusions.

TIPS ON CONDUCTING AGENT EXAMINATIONS

Finding the Time

General agents and agency managers who have limited administrative support or who have administrative support that is not qualified to help conduct examinations often find that conducting examinations is a significant challenge. Though the simplest strategy is to stop everything else until the examinations are completed, it is the least practical one. General agents and agency managers can do the following to help find the time and support for conducting agent examinations:

- Set an examination schedule and stick to it. Do not keep putting off examinations or they will all have to be done at the end of the year. This may overload the agency or office's capability to carry them out.

- Develop as streamlined an examination process as possible. Find ways to accomplish parts of the examination through self-report questionnaires rather than interviews. Have all information that can be collected and assessed in advance pulled together. Ask agents and administrative staff to help develop ways to streamline the process.

- Delegate any parts of the examination that can be effectively carried out by administrative staff. Train the administrative staff and provide them with proper tools. The general agent or agency manager should periodically review the process used by administrative staff so that he or she is confident their review is accurate.

- Pick a historically slow time in the agency or office so that everyone involved can concentrate on getting the examinations done. Allowing time for pre-examination preparation makes this concentrated effort more effective.

- Try to conduct the examinations on a weekend or using administrative staff overtime.

- Hire someone to do the examination. A retired agent might be willing to supplement income by doing examinations.

Making Follow-Through Effective

The examination is not an end in itself. Its purpose is to help identify and resolve potential issues. Some general agents and agency managers find follow-through a challenge. Here are some tips to help make follow-through more effective:

- The agent deserves personal feedback on the results of his or her examination. If the general agent or agency manager does not provide this feedback, he or she can unwittingly undermine the process. An examination should not be just aimed at finding potential issues. It also should reinforce correct procedures and provide direction on how to continue to be compliance with company procedures. An effective examination process helps agents improve the effectiveness and efficiency of their efforts to comply.

- An examination often requires follow-up on what was learned and the development of an action plan to resolve potential issues. Failure to take action on a potential market conduct issue or administrative impropriety gives the appearance that it is an accepted practice. The general agent or agency manager should develop a list of typical actions he or she would take for the most common problems. This can simplify the process of providing feedback to the agents and taking action.

- If issues are identified, the general agent or agency manager should follow-up in a reasonable period of time to make certain the agent is taking appropriate action to resolve them. The general agent or agency manager should create a schedule of examinations and follow-up dates that he or she can use to keep track of what must be accomplished.

IN CLOSING

Now that you've completed this course, you should have a good grasp on the issues surrounding compliance and some proven strategies to help you implement more effective compliance management in your day-to-day operations. As more high-profile compliance cases come to light, the importance of a well-documented, consistently implemented code of procedure and conduct for every business is hard to ignore. But far from simply avoiding penalties, we hope to have shown you how managing compliance can be a positive force for improving your business and can contribute to the overall success of your agency or office.

Appendix A:
Example of a Supervisory Responsibility Matrix

The following supervisory responsibility matrix is provided to demonstrate what such a matrix would look like. It is not intended as an all-inclusive example of the responsibilities of a general agent or agency manager.

	Company			
	ABC Mutual		*DEF Financial*	
Compliance Responsibility	*Information*	*Frequency—Responsible Party*	*Information*	*Frequency—Responsible Party*
Ensure all applications are completed accurately. Ensure all signatures are valid and appropriate. Ensure all alterations, changes and modifications of applications are appropriate. Ensure all applications contain the required forms.	N/A	Daily—Admin.	N/A	Daily—Admin.
Evaluate the suitability of sales before submission of applications.	ABC Suitability Red Flag Guidelines	Daily—GA/Admin.	DEF New Client Profile Review Checklist	Daily—GA/Admin.
Ensure that all mandated forms and guides are provided to the client at the appropriate point in the sales process.	ABC Client Disclosure Checklist	Daily—Admin.	N/A	Daily—Admin.

Appendix A: Example of a Supervisory Responsibility Matrix

	Company			
	ABC Mutual		DEF Financial	
Compliance Responsibility	Information	Frequency—Responsible Party	Information	Frequency—Responsible Party
Review all transactions involving policy values, e.g., loans or withdrawals, to ensure that they are appropriate.	N/A	Daily—Admin.	N/A	N/A
Ensure that only up-to-date company sales materials are used by agency personnel.	ABC On Line Catalog—Recent Changes Listing	Weekly—Admin.	DEF Monthly Sales Update Notice	Monthly—Admin.
Ensure that all agency personnel have copies of the most up-to-date company policies and procedures manuals.	ABC Web Site—Weekly Update, ABC Quarterly Operations Bulletin	Weekly—Admin.	DEF Monthly Sales Update Notice	Monthly—Admin.
Maintain an up-to-date agency file of all company policies and procedures.	ABC Web Site—Weekly Update, ABC Quarterly Operations Bulletin	Weekly—Admin.	DEF Monthly Sales Update Notice	Monthly—Admin.
Maintain up-to-date Do Not Call Lists and ensure that they are used.	ABC Do Not Call List Updates—DNC-28	Weekly—Admin.	DEF Do Not Call List Updates—TCL8	Weekly—Admin.
Notify the company immediately of all inquires by regulatory agencies, state regulators, SEC, NASD or IRS.	N/A	As needed—GA	N/A	As needed—GA
Identify and take appropriate action on improper agent and administrative staff behavior in a timely and appropriate manner.	N/A	As needed—GA	N/A	As needed—GA
Facilitate obtaining up-to-date information pertaining to medical status, e.g., attending physician reports.	N/A	As needed—Admin.	N/A	As needed—Admin.

Appendix A: Example of a Supervisory Responsibility Matrix

Compliance Responsibility	Company			
	ABC Mutual		DEF Financial	
	Information	*Frequency— Responsible Party*	*Information*	*Frequency— Responsible Party*
Conduct investigations of agent activities as needed under the direction of the company.	N/A	As needed— GA	N/A	As needed— GA
Review all recommendations for replacements before submitting an application and take appropriate action.	ABC Replacement Checklist— A1259	As needed— GA	N/A	N/A
Handle all written and verbal complaints according to company policy and procedure.	N/A	As needed— GA	N/A	As needed— GA
Assure that recruits complete all required information on applications and company forms before submitting the forms to the home office.	Agency recruiting and selection checklist	As needed— GA	DEF recruiting and selection package checklist	As needed— GA
Handle all initial licensing requirements, e.g., ensuring classroom training takes place.	Agency recruiting and selection checklist	As needed— GA	DEF recruiting and selection package checklist	As needed— GA
Determine that potential agents meet state, resident and nonresident licensing requirements before submitting the application to the company.	Agency recruiting and selection checklist	As needed— GA	DEF recruiting and selection package checklist	As needed— GA
Maintain a correspondence file and submit the file on a monthly basis.	N/A	N/A	N/A	Monthly—GA
Review administrative procedures, e.g., file maintenance, review of applications	N/A	Quarterly— GA	N/A	Quarterly— GA
Coach and counsel agency personnel regarding compliance and market conduct issues.	Productivity Planning Reviews	Quarterly— GA	Not Required	N/A

Appendix A: Example of a Supervisory Responsibility Matrix

	Company			
	ABC Mutual		**DEF Financial**	
Compliance Responsibility	*Information*	*Frequency— Responsible Party*	*Information*	*Frequency— Responsible Party*
Conduct regular monitoring of all company-identified issues and risks, e.g., replacements, sales to seniors, annuities in IRAs, etc.	ABC Consolidated Compliance Report—Q32-18	Quarterly— GA	Not Required	N/A
Maintain all monitoring reports in the agency's compliance file.	N/A	Quarterly— Admin.	N/A	Quarterly— Admin.
Conduct periodic audits to determine that all agency personnel have up-to-date copies of company policies and procedures manuals.	DEF File Review Checklist	Annual—GA	DEF File Review Checklist	Annual—DEF Reg. Principal
Develop individually tailored developmental action programs for all personnel whose activities warrant additional training and education in compliance and market conduct.	Annual Agent Productivity Planning Session	Annual—GA	Not Required	N/A
Conduct the annual agency compliance meeting.	ABC Agency Meeting Script/Video	Annual—GA	Annual Compliance Meeting	DEF Reg. Principal
Ensure that all agents complete mandated training requirements, e.g., pre-contract, new agent, experienced agent and advanced.	Agency annual education plan, annual agent productivity planning sessions	Annual—GA	Agency annual education plan, annual agent productivity planning sessions	Annual—GA

Appendix B:
Examples of Compliance-Related Activities

Following are examples of compliance and market conduct related activities that general agents and agency mangers may be responsible for based on their relationship with a company. This list is not inclusive of all potential activities and is provided as an example to facilitate a general agent or agency manager completing a responsibility matrix.

AGENT COMPENSATION

- Explain compensation policies by product, including compensation rules for replacements.
- Request special handling of commission payments.
- Determine bonuses and levels of support payments.
- Determine propriety of commission splitting arrangements.
- Ensure that administrative staff who are not licensed are not paid commissions.
- Explain compensation recapture rules for sales which are reversed because of compliance issues.

COMPANY AWARDS AND HONORS

- Nominate agents and administrative staff for company honors and recognition.
- Determine who will attend company meetings and conferences.
- Inform the company of agents' qualifications for company honors.

■ LICENSING, APPOINTMENT AND CONTRACTS

- Ensure that recruits complete all required information on applications and company forms before submitting the forms to the home office.

- Handle all initial licensing requirements, e.g., ensuring classroom training takes place.

- Determine that potential agents meet state, resident and nonresident licensing requirements before submitting the application to the company.

- Monitor renewal licensing requirements and alert agents to renewal deadlines.

- Review agency personnel license status semi-annually.

- Ensure that all agents have proper and up-to-date errors and omissions coverage.

- Carry out termination procedures with agents whose contracts are terminated.

- Ensure that all administrative staff members who are involved in the solicitation of insurance are properly licensed before sales are made or commissions are paid.

- Determine that applications are submitted only by brokers who are properly licensed and appointed before the sale.

■ THE SALES PROCESS

- Ensure that the appropriate level of fact finding takes place during sales.

- Review a sample of sales to determine that an appropriate needs selling approach was used.

- Evaluate the suitability of sales before submission of applications.

- Review cases to determine that illustrations are used appropriately.

- Ensure that the features, benefits and costs of products and services are disclosed properly during the sales process.

- Ensure that all mandated forms and guides are provided to the client at the appropriate point in the sales process.

- Ensure that agents and administrative staff do not provide legal or tax advice without providing the proper disclaimers and cautions.

- Maintain up-to-date do-not-call-lists and ensure that they are used.

■ THE UNDERWRITING PROCESS

- Ensure that all applications are completed accurately.
- Ensure that all signatures are valid and appropriate.
- Facilitate obtaining up-to-date information pertaining to medical status, e.g., attending physician reports.
- Ensure that all alterations, changes and modifications of applications are appropriate.
- Ensure that all applications contain the required forms.

■ COMPANY POLICIES AND PROCEDURES

- Ensure that all agency personnel have copies of the most up-to-date company policies and procedures manuals.
- Maintain an up-to-date agency file of all company policies and procedures.
- Conduct periodic audits to determine that all agency personnel have current copies of company policies and procedures manuals.
- Implement procedures to ensure that company policies and procedures are complied with.

■ HANDLING OF MONEY

- Monitor that commingling of funds is not taking place.
- Ensure that funds are transferred to the company properly.
- Ensure that all client and company monies are properly accounted for.
- Ensure that potential instances of money laundering are identified and reported promptly to the company and the proper authorities.

■ POLICY OWNER SERVICE

- Ensure that all policies are delivered to clients in a timely manner, that all free look provisions are disclosed and that all agents obtain delivery receipts.
- Investigate files to determine that clients' policies are not being retained by agents.
- Ensure that requests for changes are processed in a timely manner.
- Require agents to conduct periodic reviews of their clients' financial situations.

- Review all transaction involving policy values, such as loans or withdrawals, to ensure that they are appropriate.

- Handle all written and verbal complaints according to company policy and procedure.

PROFESSIONAL COMPETENCE

- Maintain a personal level of knowledge about compliance and market conduct policies and procedures that is sufficient to provide supervision and guidance to agents and administrative staff.

- Ensure that all agents completed mandated training requirements (e.g., pre-contract, new agent, experienced agent and advanced).

- Ensure that all management trainees and second line managers complete mandated training requirements.

- Facilitate agents, administrative staff and second line manager efforts at meeting continuing training requirements.

- Encourage agent participation in industry training and professional associations.

- Encourage agent participation in company-sponsored education and training.

- Conduct company-mandated compliance and market conduct training (e.g., the annual meeting).

- Conduct mandatory compliance training for all new hires.

ADVERTISING, SALES MATERIALS AND ILLUSTRATIONS

- Ensure that company-provided sales materials are used properly by agency personnel.

- Ensure that only up-to-date company sales materials are used by agency personnel.

- Educate agency personnel regarding the sources of company-approved sales materials.

- Ensure that only company approved sales materials are used by agency personnel.

- Review all sales material submitted for company approval before submission and only submit materials which are deemed appropriate and worthwhile.

- Conduct periodic reviews of agent sales materials to determine whether company advertising guidelines are being followed.

- Ensure that only company-approved competitive information is used by agency personnel.

- Review all incoming and outgoing correspondence and take appropriate action based on the review.

- Maintain an agency file of all sales materials used and all correspondence reviewed.

- Ensure that agency personnel do not make disparaging remarks or engage in company bashing.

REPLACEMENTS

- Ensure that all agency personnel are familiar with company and regulator replacement definitions.

- Ensure that all agency personnel follow company and regulator procedures when recommending a replacement.

- Educate agents and administrative personnel about company underwriting screening procedures for replacements.

- Review all recommendations for replacements before submitting an application and take appropriate action.

- Communicate to agents compensation policies related to replacements.

- Follow company monitoring procedures for all replacements.

MAINTAINING RECORDS

- Ensure that all agency compliance files are current and maintained properly, e.g., maintain an agency complaint log.

- Conduct periodic reviews of agency compliance files to determine whether they are being maintained properly.

- Educate all agency personnel regarding company file maintenance requirements.

- Conduct periodic reviews of agent files to determine whether they are being maintained properly.

■ CONFIDENTIALITY AND PRIVACY

- Educate all agency personnel regarding company policy on confidentiality of information and privacy policies and procedures.

- Post all company confidentiality and privacy policies prominently in the agency.

- Maintain policies and procedures to ensure that the confidentiality and privacy of all client and company information is safeguarded.

- Review any requests to release client or company information and approve only those that are within company guidelines.

- Retain all company records, files and materials when agents are terminated.

■ LEGAL AND REGULATORY REQUIREMENTS

- Ensure that all agency personnel abide by all company policies, applicable state rules and regulations and NASD rules and regulations.

- Communicate to all agency personnel that it is their responsibility to know and understand applicable rules and follow them at all times.

- Ensure that all agency personnel understand and comply with any order to submit to a review of agency records and books.

- Notify the company immediately of all inquires by regulatory agencies, state regulators, SEC, NASD or IRS.

■ VIOLATIONS OF COMPANY POLICY

- Use the company process for taking action on violations of company policies and procedures, including documenting all pertinent information and obtaining approval from the company.

- Notify the company of any actions taken regarding violations of company policies and procedures.

- Educate agency personnel regarding company policy prohibiting conflicts of interest, borrowing funds from clients, lending funds to clients and receiving gifts from clients.

- Ensure that agents do not engage in rebating.

ADDITIONAL SECTIONS FOR MANAGERS

Supervisory Responsibilities

- Conduct regular monitoring of all company-identified issues and risks, such as replacements, sales to seniors, annuities in IRAs, etc.

- Identify and take appropriate action on improper agent and administrative staff behavior in a timely and appropriate manner.

- Carry out supervisory duties according to company policies and procedures.

- Maintain all monitoring reports in the agency's compliance file.

- Conduct investigations of agent activities as needed under the direction of the company.

- Coach and counsel agency personnel regarding compliance and market conduct issues.

- Supervise all delegated compliance activities on a regular basis, such as file maintenance or application reviews.

- Develop individually tailored developmental action programs for all personnel whose activities warrant additional training and education in compliance and market conduct.

- Conduct the annual agency compliance meeting.

Recruiting and Selection

- Recruit only qualified agent candidates.

- Use the company selection standards before submitting a candidate for appointment.

- Personally interview and evaluate all agent candidates.

- Review the qualifications of all administrative before an employment offer being made.

Appendix C:
Sample Statement of Agent Conduct

ABC AGENCY INSURANCE AGENT'S CODE OF CONDUCT

Our agency's success can be attributed to the quality of the business sold by its agents and the excellent service they and their administrative staff provide to our clients. To preserve our reputation for quality and fair and ethical treatment of the public and our clients, these high standards must be maintained.

As an agent or administrative staff member of the ABC Agency, you are in a position of responsibility and trust. You are expected to live up to the standards in this code of conduct. In addition, you are expected to comply with the specific standards, policies and procedures of the companies with which you have a relationship. You should carefully review and have a full understanding of the ABC Agency code and the contents of the company standards, policies and procedures of the companies with which you do business.

THE SALES PROCESS

You are ABC Agency's representative in communicating complete and accurate information to clients about the companies you represent and their products and services. Your recommendations should be based on a thorough, documented analysis of your client's needs and financial objectives. Based on this information, your recommendations should be designed to satisfy those needs and objectives in a way that is appropriate and suitable for the client.

You should make every effort to ensure that clients understand the products and services you recommend. Do not omit or misrepresent important information to mislead the client. You should state the exact nature of the features and benefits of the products and services you present accurately. You should provide full disclosure of all pertinent obligations, conditions, charges, fees, requirements, etc., pertaining to the products and services you recommend so that prospective clients can make informed and intelligent decisions. You should use only appropriate and approved sales materials to inform and educate consumers about the products and services you are recommending.

THE UNDERWRITING PROCESS

Once a prospective client has decided to proceed with a purchase, your role is to provide complete, pertinent and accurate information about the prospective client to the home office underwriters of the company with which you are placing the business, so they can effectively perform their evaluation and selection function. Withholding or misrepresenting information that could affect the decision process (e.g., smokers, pre-existing medical conditions, age, insurance need or ability to pay) would be considered unacceptable, irresponsible conduct on the part of the agent involved. It would not only cast doubt on the specific risk in question, but also would raise serious issues about the credibility of past and future business transactions processed by such an agent. Any alterations, changes, additions, deletions, etc. in the application must be appropriately initialed by the applicant. Multiple changes in applications may require that a new application be taken.

Once the application has been submitted, but before it has been delivered, if you learn of any information that would affect the underwriting process, you must communicate that information to the company to which your have sent the application in a timely manner.

SIGNATURES

For companies to rely on the authenticity of every signature they receive, agents must never sign on behalf of applicants, doctors, beneficiaries or anyone else on any company document.

HANDLING MONEY

Every agent of the ABC Agency must know and respect the difference between his or her personal funds, the insured's money, the beneficiary's money and ABC Agency's money. In addition, the payment of premiums by an agent on behalf of a client is not acceptable in any form. In most cases, premium payments should not be accepted in cash without prior authorization from the company providing the product.

POLICYHOLDER SERVICE

As a representative of the ABC Agency, your service role continues after the sale to your client. This includes the prompt delivery of all policies and a full explanation of any free look provisions that may apply. Where required by state regulation or specific company policy, agents must obtain a signed and dated policy delivery receipt. Even when not required, it is recommended that you obtain a receipt or otherwise document that the policy was delivered.

Generally, you should not retain a client's policy in your possession for safekeeping or other purposes. If requested by the client, you should document the request and then obtain written authorization from the company providing the product to retain a copy.

All policyholder requests for changes and financial transactions (changes of address, changes of premium mode, policy loans, surrenders, dividend withdrawals, etc.) must be processed efficiently and properly, and include appropriate documentation as required by the company providing the product.

The ABC Agency General Agent must be given all written complaints received by agents or administrative staff within 24 hours of receipt. The General Agent then will forward the complaint to the appropriate company's home office. A written complaint is any written document expressing a grievance against an agent, an administrative staff person, the agency or a company represented by the agent by a policyholder, client, beneficiary or their legal representative, or a regulatory agency such as a state insurance department.

PROFESSIONAL COMPETENCE

To properly carry out your responsibilities as a member of the ABC Agency, you are expected to acquire and maintain the knowledge and skills required to provide sound professional advice about the products and services you provide and their use in helping clients fulfill their financial needs and objectives. You are expected to participate in professional training and education and to continue your development throughout your career.

LICENSING

Before soliciting insurance applications for any of the companies you represent, you are expected to hold and maintain the appropriate licenses and satisfy state and NASD laws and regulations regarding licensing and appointment. You are expected to determine whether your administrative staff requires licensing to carry out their duties and to ensure that they are properly licensed and appointment before becoming involved in the solicitation of insurance applications.

ADVERTISING, SALES MATERIALS AND ILLUSTRATIONS

All advertisements and materials involved in or related to the sale of a product or service or which contain or refer to any company with which you have a contractual relationship must be approved in advance of their use and in writing by the company who is mentioned. You must only use company-approved sales materials when presenting a company's products and services. This includes, but is not limited to, newspaper and magazine ads, stationery, business cards, brochures, direct mail and pre-approach letters, sales presentations, seminar presentations, sales scripts, radio and television spots, etc. The use of the Internet for marketing products and services is subject to the same polices and procedures as written or printed materials.

Comparative or competitive information must be approved in advance by the company whose product is being presented like any other form of sales material. Comparisons must be true, current and factual.

Illustrations can be of value in helping clients understand how insurance products and services can help them fulfill their needs and financial objectives. Only company-approved illustrations of products may be shown to clients. Any sales material or correspondence which presents numerical information or data about guaranteed or non-guaranteed elements of an insurance product is considered an illustration and must be approved before use. States differ with respect to their requirements for illustrations. You are expected to follow all rules and regulations pertaining to illustrations based on the jurisdictions in which you operate.

You must never show the public any materials identified as For Internal Use Only, For Broker-Dealer Use Only, etc. You may not use all or part of this material with the public without company permission.

FAIR COMPETITION

State regulations prohibit agents from making disparaging or untrue oral or written statements about other agents or companies. You are expected to avoid making comments that are deceptive, misleading, or derogatory about competitors. You should exercise care that any statements made about competitors are factual, up-to-date and substantiated.

REPLACEMENTS

Replacement as defined by state regulations includes any transaction where existing insurance has been or will be lapsed, forfeited, surrendered or terminated or reduced in value by use of policy values. Reductions in value can include, but are not limited to: conversion to reduced paid up insurance, reissued with a reduction in cash value, borrowing greater than 25 percent of the loan value to purchase additional coverage, using the policy values to pay future premiums on the existing policy, etc. You must be familiar with the replacement regulations of the jurisdictions in which you operate and abide by them.

Replacement of existing policies should occur only when it is in the best interest of the client with appropriate disclosure as required by state regulations. You must disclose all of the advantages and disadvantages of the replacement to the client. The client must fully understand the financial consequences of this action and, where required by regulation or industry practice, agree to it in writing.

You must indicate on the application for the new coverage whenever a replacement is involved in a sale.

MAINTAINING RECORDS

Accurate and reliable records are necessary to meet both your professional and contractual responsibilities. Because of this, you are expected to keep up-to-date records and files of all transactions, correspondence, documentation, etc.

You are expected to make your records available to the General Agent and a company for the purpose of auditing or conducting any regulatory or administrative examination of the ABC Agency or the company.

■ **CONFIDENTIALITY AND PRIVACY**

In your role as an agent of the ABC Agency, you will possess confidential information about your clients and the agency and the companies you represent. A breach of confidentiality can have serious consequences. You must safeguard all confidential client, beneficiary, company, etc., information and only provide access to individuals who have a legitimate right to it. You are responsible for maintaining the security of all confidential information in your possession. Before providing information or using information for marketing purposes, you should review the policies of the companies your represent and the agency policy described in the ABC Agency Privacy and Confidentiality Policy.

■ **LEGAL AND REGULATORY REQUIREMENTS**

It is ABC Agency policy to operate within the framework of all state, federal and regulatory bodies' (e.g., NASDR) laws, rules and regulations governing the sale of products and services of the companies we represent. You are expected to abide by all rules and regulations governing the sale of our products specific to the jurisdictions in which you do business. You also are expected to be knowledgeable about these rules and regulations and alert to changes in them.

■ **VIOLATIONS OF COMPANY POLICY**

The purpose of the ABC Agency's policies and procedures is to provide the highest quality products and services to its clients and agents. You are expected to abide by the policies and procedures of the companies you represent. To protect the ABC Agency's reputation and the good name and reputation of all of our agents and the companies with which we do business, the ABC Agency and the company involved will take action on any violations of policies or procedures. These actions will be related directly to the seriousness of the violation and its consequences. Actions may range from verbal warnings to termination of contacts or, in appropriate cases, prosecution.

Appendix D:
The Concept of Ethical Leadership

WHAT IS ETHICAL LEADERSHIP?

The starting point to understanding ethical leadership is your values. The values of honesty, integrity, holding people responsible for their actions, fairness, etc., are the values that a general agent or agency manager must have to be an ethical leader. But, much more is needed. *Ethical leadership is values in action.* A listing of values is unimportant in defining ethical leadership. Only a list of actions can adequately define ethical leadership.

Ethical Leadership	*Unethical Leadership*
Applies high ethical standards to everyone.	Is willing to compromise standards based on the situation—top agents are held to a different standard.
Uses clients' welfare and doing what's best for the public as the primary standard.	Uses the company's, their own or the agent's welfare—doing what's best for them—as the primary standard.
Confronts situations where ethics are questionable.	Is unwilling to confront ethical issues unless they are safe, uncomplicated and lack risk or he or she is forced to confront them by the company or regulators.
Takes timely and appropriate action on ethical issues.	Avoids taking action on ethical issues in favor of expediency, or seeks to soften the blow by minimizing the impact. Takes action only when forced to.
Heads off ethical problems.	Does not deal with ethical issues until there is an obvious and significant problem.
Confronts ethical issues openly and honestly.	Does not want to make ethics an issue. Ignores ethical issues or deals with them covertly.
Leads by example, treats ethics as a priority.	Downplays the importance of ethics, treats it as a nice to do, not a must do.
Acknowledges that our industry has not done enough on a consistent basis to prevent the current industry problems—sees ethics as a company, management and individual responsibility.	Blames villains—other companies, class action attorneys, rogue agents and others for the current industry problems-sees ethics as an individual responsibility.
Does the right thing and is concerned about the right thing to do rather than doing the legal minimum.	Is concerned about legal liability and blame more than the right thing to do.
Treats ethics as a performance measure no different than sales, and actively supervises it.	Seeks to minimize his or her personal responsibility for supervision of ethical issues and behavior.
Learns about the legal and ethical aspects of the business and does not plead ignorance when asked a question.	Ignores the legal and ethical aspects of the business, pleads ignorance of the issues and the regulations.
Does not use other companies' lower standards as an excuse.	Sets his or her standard at the lowest level of the competition and uses as an excuse that other companies are not taking as high a standard.
Rewards, recognizes and praises individuals who work to improve compliance and market conduct.	Denigrates or punishes efforts to improve compliance and market conduct.

WHY ETHICAL LEADERSHIP IS IMPORTANT

Because general agents and agency managers are in a position of authority and responsibility in an agency or office, a lack of ethical leadership can place everyone in the agency or office at risk. General agents and agency managers who do not exercise ethical leadership can inadvertently create serious compliance and market conduct problems by unwittingly communicating to their agents and administrative staff that compliance and market conduct is not important and that misconduct will be tolerated. If they ignore potential problems or excuse inappropriate behavior, in the long run, they and their agents may pay a high price.

General agents and agency managers who do not display ethical leadership may also derail a company's attempts to improve the compliance and market conduct of the agents they have a relationship with. General agents and agency managers who lack ethical leadership may fail to spend the time and energy needed to implement enhancements to company compliance and market conduct policies, procedures and programs.

A general agent or agency manager who is not an ethical leader cannot fake it through loud pronouncements. His or her agents and administrative staff often can see through that. When a general agent or agency manager makes a speech at a meeting about the importance of compliance, but then praises an agent who is known to be a shady character, it becomes clear that he or she is exhibiting unethical leadership. When he or she overlooks or excuses the compliance problems of top agents, it tells the agency or office that ethical behavior is not important. Finally, when he or she actively courts experienced agents who have a reputation for being replacement artists, the message is louder than any comments about high standards. As a role model, a general agent or agency manager's lack of ethical leadership will serve as a standard for his or her associates. No industry or company program can overcome that.

One of the problems with ethical leadership is that *there is no middle ground.* A general agent or agency manager is the leader of an agency or office. As the leader of the agency or office, he or she either is an ethical leader or an unethical one. His or her actions demonstrate one of two paths for others to follow. If they signal that unethical behavior is acceptable, then the standard is set for others. Therefore, one of the most important roles a general agent or agency manager can play is to provide ethical leadership to his or her associates.

Appendix E:
Being out of Compliance Is Bad for Business—An Agent's Perspective

Complying with the rules and regulations formulated by the states, federal government and other regulatory agencies is the easiest way to avoid legal and ethical problems. Agents have much to lose if they fail to comply. The increased scrutiny of state regulators, as well as increased public awareness and sensitivity, means that unethical practices are more likely than ever to become known.

We live in a litigious society. Every profession has become the target of disgruntled consumers and their legal counsel. The insurance industry is no exception. Over the last several years some of the most prestigious insurance companies have found themselves in the cross hairs of plaintiffs' counsel.

Agents suffer when they are the targets of lawsuits or compliance and market conduct problems. Following are some of the costs of improper market conduct:

- **Reputation.** Your name is your fame! Reputation often is a key to success. Top agents prospect via referrals, and if your name is dirtied in local communities, you might as well close up shop. Even when you are found to have done nothing wrong, accusations of misconduct are hard to erase in people's minds, regardless of the outcome. Being the target of a lawsuit based on an allegation of improper market conduct often is difficult to keep confidential. Usually, you cannot keep it a secret from other professionals or from your local community. There are a number of ways that the information gets out. For example, a company may be required to survey other clients of yours to check for similar problems are present. Or the state may request that other clients be interviewed to assess your practices. Though they will not blatantly ask your clients to identify sales practices, it is fairly apparent from the questions they ask that they are.

- **Time.** Nothing eats up productive time like a market conduct problem: responding to written requests for information from the company or state regulators, interviews with your company's E&O carrier's legal counsel, reviews of your files, preparing for and giving depositions, etc. Time spent on unproductive activities cannot be reclaimed: Furthermore, cases often take a long time to run their course—many going on for years. Much time is spent reviewing material over and over again as each new stage in the legal process takes place.

- **Self-confidence.** Your self-confidence suffers when you find yourself under the gun in a lawsuit or the subject of a market conduct investigation. Even if you win, you carry the scars of self-doubt. You wonder what else can come back to haunt you. The specter of a market conduct problem hanging over your head, even if you feel you have nothing to fear, often impacts an agent's self-confidence. Even if you know you did nothing wrong, you have been accused and it often makes one wonder.

- **Trust in your client's motivation.** When a client you trusted accuses you of wrong doing, it is only natural to question the motivations of all of your clients. Agents who have been accused of market conduct errors often become very cynical about their clients and the seemingly close relationship they have. You may find yourself asking, is this another person who will try to get me, if things do not go right?

- **Company trust in the agent.** When an company thinks an agent may have done something wrong, it must scrutinize the agent's business. Companies will be cautious of agents who have been the target of market conduct complaints because that proper supervision requires them to pay attention in dealing with such agents. Companies may be less willing to make exceptions in policies and procedures for agents who have been accused of improper market conduct, let alone ones who have been found guilty of acting improperly.

- **Confidence in your associates.** If you work with other insurance, financial planning, legal or business professionals, their confidence in your advice could be weakened if you are the target of a misconduct charge. Would you want to work on a case with someone was accused of having improper market conduct?

What if you are found to have done something wrong? It is probably unthinkable, but it does happen. Sometimes the problem is minor but is blown out of proportion by a plaintiff's attorney. Sometimes it is something the agent did for the client, like overestimating net worth or not digging deep enough when filling out the application. If a variable product is involved, the company will report the misconduct to the NASD and likely will fine the agent. This is on your record and will hinder your ability to move to a new broker-dealer. If it is a serious problem, it may result in loss of NASD registration for a period. Fines levied by the NASD must be paid by the individual fined. A complaint will be reported to any company you are seeking a new contract with. It may cause them to think twice about extending a contract to you. If the company terminates your contract, you must report it when you seek out other carriers. If clients in your book of business need help on their policies, you cannot service them because the company will not give you software, updates, information or in some cases even listen to you. And if you start to roll over your business, they may sue you. You cannot split commissions if one of your associates still works with them.

Appendix F:
Listing of Potential Examination Points

The following list of examination points is provided as a sample. It does not represent all possible examination points. Other examination points may be required to fully examine the market conduct and compliance of an agency or office depending on company and regulator requirements. For each examination point, the company would develop a procedure for collecting, evaluating and documenting the results of the examination.

GENERAL

- Are all agents and managers licensed in the state in which they do business?

- Are administrative staff members who solicit business licensed?

- Are signed agent and manager contracts on file at the company home office for all active personnel?

- Does every registered representative have a current U-4?

- Are any complaints on file at the company home office against any agent, administrative staff member or manager? Is there a pattern to the complaints?

- Does the general agent or agency manager have any individuals in training to become agents? If yes, has any agent in training been contracted for more than 90 days?

- Has any agent in training written any business other than with a member of management or another licensed agent?

- Which agents have joined the company since the last examination?

- Do all agents and managers have proof of current E&O coverage?

- What products typically are sold? What typical market conduct issues are related to these products?

- In which markets are sales typically made? What typical market conduct issues are related to these markets?

- What is the overall level of persistency? How does it differ from company, agency or office averages?

  - Which agents have the highest persistency, which the lowest?

- What is the overall level of replacement activity? How does it differ from company, agency or office averages?

  - Which agents have the highest number of internal replacements and the highest percentage of sales commissions involving internal replacements?

  - Which agents have the highest number of external replacements and the highest percentage of sales commissions involving external replacements?

- What were the results of prior examinations? What action plans were agreed to and what follow-up was provided?

AGENCY OR OFFICE ADMINISTRATION

- Does the agency or office's master compliance file contain copies of approved:

  - applications;

  - disclosure forms;

  - fact finders;

  - needs analysis forms;

  - risk assessment documentation;

  - written client report templates;

  - sales presentation materials, such as paper and computer based systems;

  - illustration software;

  - advertising, e.g., telephone directory templates, signage, etc.;

  - sales materials, brochures, etc.;

  - up-to-date listings of approved sales materials and advertising;

  - new client forms;

- up-to-date Do Not Call List;
- state-required forms and materials, e.g., buyer's guides for all states in which the agency or office does business;
- company-required forms; and
- delivery receipts.

- Is the material in the agent or office's master compliance file up-to-date?
  - Has the file been maintained since the last examination?

- Are agency or office files restricted to anyone?

- Are all confidential files maintained in locked cabinets?

- Does the manager's compliance communications file contain:
  - all current compliance and market conduct communications, information, updates, memos, etc.;
  - all agent, administrative staff, general agent and agency manager manuals, guides, etc.;
  - documentation of communication of information to agents and staff (e.g., receipts or acknowledgments);
  - evidence that compliance and market conduct communications, information, etc. is shared with agents and staff; and
  - copies of the company code of ethics readily available.

- Is the material in the general agent or agency manager's compliance communications file up-to-date? Has the file been maintained since the last examination?

- Does the general agent or agency manager's training file contain:
  - copies of all agent, administrative staff and manager training materials, e.g., company training or NASD firm element continuing education;
  - a training log (i.e., documentation of when, how and to whom training was provided);
  - copies of acknowledgments required as part of training programs; and
  - information on continuing education requirements for the states in which the agency or office does business.

- Are managers, service staff and agents knowledgeable about company compliance and market conduct policies and procedures (e.g., complaint handling, replacements, sales material review, etc.)?

- Are sales materials for agent use kept in a location where they are always available? What are the controls for access?

- Are sales materials (e.g., prospectus) kept up-to-date?

- Are company procedures followed in handling complaints? Is the proper complaint log maintained and up-to-date?

- Are company and state procedures followed in sales involving replacements? Is the proper replacement log maintained and up-to-date?

- Is the office telephone answered properly?

- Is company-related signage appropriate?

- Does management review new business applications for:

  - suitability;

  - replacements; and

  - proper signatures.

- Does management maintain and periodically review complaint, persistency, replacement, etc. reports?

- Has management delegated compliance and market conduct responsibility to anyone else in the office? Is that person qualified to carry out the delegated responsibility?

- Has management taken appropriate action on market conduct and compliance issues?

- Does management demonstrate support of company compliance policies and procedures?

- If the manager is a registered principal, does he or she maintain an agent review file that contains a review schedule and the results of all reviews?

- If the office maintains the daily sales log or blotter for registered product sales, is it up-to-date?

AGENT FILES

- Do client files contain copies of:

  - applications

  - disclosure forms

  - fact finders

- needs-analysis forms
- risk assessment documentation
- sales materials provided to clients
- required sales materials
- optional sales materials
- correspondence
- illustrations
- new client forms
- state-required forms
- company-required forms
- delivery receipts
- policy summary sheets

- Does the file contain any policies or contracts other than those recently issued and pending delivery? If yes, has written authorization to do so been obtained from the company's home office?

- Were company procedures followed in sales involving replacements?

- Does the agent's computer have only approved software loaded?

- Does a review of a sample of client files indicate any potential market conduct issues?

- If the agent is a registered representative, does he or she maintain a separate correspondence to be reviewed file? Is the file up-to-date?

- If the agent is a registered representative, does he or she maintain a daily sales log, file or blotter? Is the log current?

Appendix G:
Sample of an NASD Examination Record Form

Following is a sample of an examination questionnaire record form for use with a registered representative. Its purpose is to guide and document an on-site examination. It is not meant to serve as a model. Broker-dealers tailor their questionnaires to fit their representatives' markets, their products and their supervisory structure. This questionnaire is provided for illustrative purposes only.

Section 1—Personal Data

1. Agent Name _____ Contract No. _____

2. Agent Business Address: ☐ Agency/Office   ☐ Other:

   _____
   Street   City   State   Zip

   _____
   Street   City   State   Zip

3. Agent Phone No. _____ Fax No. _____

4. Agent E-Mail Address: _____

5. Agent Web Site Address: _____

6. Agent NASD Registrations (check all that apply):   ☐ ABC Financial   ☐ Other

   Comment(s): _____

7. Agent certifications (check all that apply) ☐ CLU   ☐ ChFC
   ☐ CFP   ☐ MSFS   ☐ RHU   ☐ Other (list)

   _____

8. Administrative Staff Name(s):
   a. _____ Lic/State: _____
   b. _____ Lic/State: _____
   c. _____ Lic/State: _____

Other Pertinent Personal Information: _____
_____

Section 2—Site Inspection

1. Is the agent licensed in all states where clients reside?

   ☐ Yes   ☐ No (List all states where licenses currently are held.)_____
   _____

2. a. Resident state CE reporting period end date: _____
   b. Number of credits required: _____
   c. Number of credits completed in the current reporting period: _____
   (Attach an additional sheet if necessary.)

3. Do stationery/business cards meet ABC Financial (ABCF) requirements?

   ☐ Yes   ☐ No (Comment) _____

4. Does the fax cover sheet meet ABCF requirements?

   ☐ Yes   ☐ No (Comment) _____

5. Does the agent's typical sales process utilize materials that were approved in advance by ABCF's Compliance Department?

   ☐ Yes   ☐ No (Comment) _____

6. Do business checks and account titles avoid references to ABCF?

   ☐ Yes   ☐ No (Comment) _____

7. Do telephone and voicemail greetings meet ABCF requirements?

   ☐ Yes   ☐ No (Comment) _____

8. Do the initial screens of the agent's web site meet ABCF requirements?

   ☐ Yes   ☐ No (Comment) _____

9. Do phone directory listings meet ABCF requirements?

   ☐ Yes   ☐ No (Comment) _____

10. Does office signage (e.g., building directory) meet ABCF requirements?

    ☐ Yes   ☐ No (Comment) _____

11. Is the agent's office clearly distinguishable and sufficiently separated from the entrance to any nearby financial services offices?

    ☐ Yes   ☐ No (Comment) _____

12. Are the ABCF logo, broker-dealer name, company addresses, 800 telephone number and web site address prominently displayed in the office?

    ☐ Yes   ☐ No (Comment) _____

13. Is the ABCF Statement of Ethics prominently displayed in the office?

    ☐ Yes   ☐ No (Comment) _____

14. Is a current version of the ABCF Registered Representative Manual present in the office?

    ☐ Yes   ☐ No (Comment) _____

15. Is a current version of the ABCF Guide to Compliance and Market Conduct present in the office?

    ☐ Yes   ☐ No (Comment) _____

Section 3—Records Review

1. Is a signed copy of Responsibilities of Being an ABCF Representative, dated within the last 12 months, present in the agency/office files?

    ☐ Yes   ☐ No (Comment) _____

2. Does the agent have an up-to-date and complete file of all past issues of ABCF's Registered Representative Updates?

    ☐ Yes   ☐ No (Comment) _____

3. Is the agent's supply of variable contact prospectuses, offering circulars, separate account updates, client account forms and variable product sales materials current?

    ☐ Yes   ☐ No (Comment) _____

4. Does the agent maintain the following:

Correspondence log	☐ Yes	☐ No
Complaint log	☐ Yes	☐ No
Sales blotter	☐ Yes	☐ No
Policy delivery log	☐ Yes	☐ No
Advertising review log	☐ Yes	☐ No
Web site contact log	☐ Yes	☐ No
Sales material update listing	☐ Yes	☐ No
Do Not Call List	☐ Yes	☐ No
Compliance communication log	☐ Yes	☐ No
An up-to-date copy of the U-4	☐ Yes	☐ No

    (Comment) _____

5. Are appropriate copies present in client files of the following (based on a review of a sample of five current client files):

Fact finder/data taker	☐ Yes	☐ No
Needs analysis report	☐ Yes	☐ No
New client form	☐ Yes	☐ No
Risk assessment documentation	☐ Yes	☐ No

Client acknowledgment form	☐ Yes	☐ No
Mutual commitment form	☐ Yes	☐ No
Illustration	☐ Yes	☐ No
List of sales materials, brochures, etc. provided to the client	☐ Yes	☐ No
Delivery receipt	☐ Yes	☐ No
Replacement forms	☐ Yes	☐ No
Client contact log	☐ Yes	☐ No
Meeting notes	☐ Yes	☐ No

(Comment) _____
_____

6. Are any client information or records maintained in electronic form?

   ☐ Yes   ☐ No (Comment) _____

7. What types of software are used on a regular basis? (Attach a separate list if necessary.) _____
_____
_____

8. Identify all computers used in the regular course of doing business and their location. (List)
_____
_____

9. List all web addresses used in the regular course of doing business.
_____
_____

10. Is there a copy of an approved web site content agreement in the representative's files?

    ☐ Yes   ☐ No (Comment) _____

Section 4—Interview

1. Do you hold yourself out to the public as anything other than a life insurance agent or a registered representative of ABCF?

   ☐ Yes   ☐ No (Comment) _____

2. Do you use with clients or prospects any advertising, illustration software, brochures or other sales materials that have not been approved by the ABCF Compliance Department before use?

   ☐ Yes   ☐ No (Comment) _____

3. Do you market variable annuities specifically to clients aged 65 or older?

   ☐ Yes   ☐ No (Comment) _____

4. Are you involved in work site marketing?

   ☐ Yes   ☐ No   If yes, describe your last two cases. _____
_____

5. In a state where the NAIC model illustration regulation is in effect, do you always give the client a corresponding basic illustration at the same time or before giving the client a supplemental illustration?

   ☐ Yes   ☐ No (Comment) _____

6. Have you read and do you understand ABCF's replacement policy?

   ☐ Yes   ☐ No (Comment) _____

7. Do you accept premium payments or loan repayments from a client in cash, money orders or traveler's checks?

   ☐ Yes   ☐ No (Comment) _____

8. Do you forward all checks and monies received on behalf of a client to the ABCF home office within 24 hours of receipt?

   ☐ Yes   ☐ No (Comment) _____

9. Have you ever used sales materials with clients that were not approved in advance by ABCF's Compliance Department?

   ☐ Yes   ☐ No (Comment) _____

10. In the past 12 months have you become involved in any outside business activities that were not first disclosed to ABCF?

    ☐ Yes   ☐ No (Comment) _____

11. Are you a trustee, director, officer, partner, etc. of any organization or business?

    ☐ Yes   ☐ No (Comment) _____

12. Are you involved in any fundraising or charitable activities involving the handling of money, investments, trusteeships, etc.?

    ☐ Yes   ☐ No (Comment) _____

13. Are you involved in any outside writing, broadcasting, or teaching activity?

    ☐ Yes   ☐ No (Comment) _____

14. In the past 12 months, have you run for and been elected to political office or been appointed to a governmental position?

    ☐ Yes   ☐ No (Comment) _____

15. In the past 12 months, have you paid any commission or production based compensation to an unregistered individual?

    ☐ Yes   ☐ No (Comment) _____

16. In the past 12 months, have you received a fee for services provided to clients?

    ☐ Yes   ☐ No (Comment) _____

17. In the past 12 months, have you forwarded all verbal and written complaints to the ABCF Compliance Department?

    ☐ Yes   ☐ No (Comment) _____

18. In the last 12 months, have you engaged in the sale of any registered product that is not distributed by ABCF or one of its affiliates?

    ☐ Yes   ☐ No (Comment) _____

19. In the past 12 months, did you have any personal accounts with other NASD broker-dealers?

    ☐ Yes   ☐ No (Comment) _____

20. In the past 12 months, have you loaned money to or borrowed money from clients?

    ☐ Yes   ☐ No (Comment) _____

21. In the past 12 months, have you made any private settlements (paying losses, charges or adjustments) with any client?

    ☐ Yes   ☐ No (Comment) _____

22. In the past 12 months, have you deposited client funds into your personal or business account or in any way commingled funds?

    ☐ Yes   ☐ No (Comment) _____

23. In the past 12 months, have you shown clients any materials marked For Internal Use Only or For Registered Representative Use Only?

    ☐ Yes   ☐ No (Comment) _____

24. In the past 12 months, have you been involved in any litigation of a criminal or civil nature?

    ☐ Yes   ☐ No (Comment) _____

25. In the past 12 months, have you been involved in any inquiry, visit, investigation, disciplinary action, etc. by a regulatory body?

    ☐ Yes   ☐ No (Comment) _____

26. In the past 12 months, have you been in receipt of a subpoena or been involved in litigation or arbitration of any kind?

    ☐ Yes   ☐ No (Comment) _____

27. In the past 12 months, have you been involved in any bankruptcy or contempt proceedings?

    ☐ Yes   ☐ No (Comment) _____

28. In the past 12 months have you received a summons or subpoena for a criminal offense? Have you been arrested, charged, fined or imprisoned for a criminal offense (excluding traffic violations)?

    ☐ Yes   ☐ No (Comment) _____

29. In the past 12 months have you been accused of conduct which violates state or NASD rules or securities laws?

    ☐ Yes   ☐ No (Comment) _____

30. In the past 12 months, have you been assessed damages that were settled for $2,500 or more?

    ☐ Yes   ☐ No (Comment) _____

Section 5—Communications with Prospects and Clients

1. Have you sent or received business-related e-mail to clients via an account other than ABCFinancial.com?

   ☐ Yes   ☐ No (Comment) _____

2. Do you receive any business-related correspondence at a post office box or similar mail handling facility?

   ☐ Yes   ☐ No (Comment) _____

3. Have you received any incoming client correspondence (including faxes) that was not first opened and reviewed by agency staff?

   ☐ Yes   ☐ No (Comment) _____

4. Do you provide copies of all incoming correspondence to your supervisor?

   ☐ Yes   ☐ No (Comment) _____

5. Has all outgoing client correspondence been reviewed and approved by your supervisor before being sent to a client?

   ☐ Yes   ☐ No (Comment) _____

6. Is all incoming correspondence date and time stamped?

   ☐ Yes   ☐ No (Comment) _____

Section 6—Signatures

I have reviewed the information on all pages of this Examination Interview form. I agree that all of my responses have been correctly recorded.

Representative Signature _____ Date _____

Reviewer Signature _____ Date _____

Appendix H:
Sample Case or File Review Checklist

Agent Sales/Marketing Activity Evaluation Checklist

For each of the following, evidence in the client file should support the affirmative answer for each item.

	Yes	No
1. Sales materials (direct mail letters, brochures, business cards, stationery, etc.) used to secure the appointment were approved by the company whose products were presented, e.g., there are company approval numbers for the materials, or approval letters on file, etc.	☐	☐
2. The agent was properly licensed, appointed and registered in the state in which the client resides to sell the products presented or recommended.	☐	☐
3. The agent provided information that identified himself or herself, the company and the purpose of the sales interview properly, e.g., business card, brochure, etc. If the agent is a registered representative, the agent provided information that identified his or her broker-dealer.	☐	☐
4. The client was not shown or given any information that was labeled for internal use only or not to be shown to the public.	☐	☐
5. Fact-finding was accomplished using an approved form and process (paper or computer).	☐	☐
6. Fact-finding covered a wide range of appropriate questions whose answers were recorded, e.g., an approved fact-finder was fully completed.	☐	☐

	Yes	*No*
7. The client's financial needs and objectives were evaluated carefully and analyzed using a documented process, e.g., a company-approved process was used.	☐	☐
8. Various types of products and services were assessed for suitability based on the client's financial objectives, needs and risk tolerance.	☐	☐
9. Recommendations for products and services to meet the client's needs and objectives were based on a logical, documented process.	☐	☐
10. The agent was knowledgeable about the recommended products and services.	☐	☐
11. The agent only used illustrations approved by the company whose product was presented, and were signed by the client, if required.	☐	☐
12. The broker-dealer's new account or new client forms were completed for registered product sales.	☐	☐
13. For registered product sales, a current prospectus, including any required supplements, was provided.	☐	☐
14. Full disclosure and a balanced presentation were provided regarding the type, operation, features and benefits of the products and services recommended.	☐	☐
15. The agent provided a receipt for any policies, contracts or documentation taken from the premises to review and evaluate.	☐	☐
16. The application and field underwriting process were completed properly and included all necessary signatures.	☐	☐
17. The state's free look provisions were described, e.g., on a disclosure form, a brochure or the application.	☐	☐
18. Copies of any state-required materials (e.g., buyer's guides) were provided, e.g., a copy of the materials was included in the file or noted or it was noted on the disclosure form.	☐	☐
19. Proper disclosures were provided regarding legal and tax advice.	☐	☐
20. If any type of replacement was recommended, extra care was taken to ensure that it was properly documented, it was in the client's best interest and the client was clearly informed that the sale involved a replacement.	☐	☐

	Yes	No
21. Required replacement forms were completed (including 1035 exchange paperwork) and signed by the client where necessary.	☐	☐
22. All company-required disclosure forms were completed and copies were given to the client (if required).	☐	☐
23. The agent did not accept cash and followed all company policies regarding initial payments.	☐	☐
24. The agent submitted the application promptly with all required paperwork.	☐	☐
25. The agent followed up on the application to ensure that it was processed in a timely manner.	☐	☐
26. If the policy was not issued as applied for, the agent met with the client and explained the reasons for the changes.	☐	☐
27. If a new illustration and disclosure were required before or at policy delivery, the illustration was provided, the proper disclosure was provided and the form was signed.	☐	☐
28. The agent obtained a signed policy delivery receipt.	☐	☐
29. The agent remained in regular contact with the client and conducted periodic reviews.	☐	☐
30. The agent maintained all required information in a client file.	☐	☐